Contemporary Issues in Special Educational Needs

Contemporary Issues in Special Educational Needs

Considering the whole child

Edited by David Armstrong and Garry Squires

Open University Press

Open University Press
McGraw-Hill Education
McGraw-Hill House
Shoppenhangers Road
Maidenhead
Berkshire
England
SL6 2QL

email: enquiries@openup.co.uk
world wide web: www.openup.co.uk

and Two Penn Plaza, New York, NY 10121-2289, USA

First published 2012

Copyright © David Armstrong and Garry Squires, 2012

A catalogue record of this book is available from the British Library

ISBN-13: 978-0-33-524363-1 (pb)
ISBN-10: 0-33-524363-0 (pb)
eISBN: 978-0-33-524365-5

Library of Congress Cataloging-in-Publication Data
CIP data applied for

Typesetting and e-book compilations by
RefineCatch Limited, Bungay, Suffolk
Printed and bound in the UK by Bell & Bain Ltd, Glasgow

Fictitious names of companies, products, people, characters and/or data that may
be used herein (in case studies or in examples) are not intended to represent any
real individual, company, product or event.

MIX
Paper from
responsible sources
FSC
www.fsc.org   FSC® C007785

The McGraw·Hill Companies

Contents

About the editors

Dr. David Armstrong
David is an independent educational consultant, having previously worked as a Senior Lecturer at Edge Hill University, Ormskirk, UK. In the past he has worked with excluded children, the homeless and adults with learning disabilities, and as a Special Educational Needs Coordinator. His research interests include the psychology of learning/psychology, language development, and mental health among young people. He is a member of the British Psychological Society (having the Graduate Basis for Chartered membership) and is a passionate believer in an ethically reformed education for children and young people.

Dr. Garry Squires
Garry is Director for the Professional Doctorate in Educational Psychology at the University of Manchester and formerly worked as an educational psychologist, providing training to teachers and psychologists in the area of SEND. He is an Associate Fellow of the British Psychological Society and is registered with the Health Professions Council as a practitioner psychologist. He brings a combined academic and practitioner perspective to this book. Garry has a number of publications in the areas of SEND and inclusion. His research is in the areas of SEN, inclusion and mental health, and has published in popular SEN magazines, peer-reviewed journals, and presented papers at UK and international conferences. He is on the editorial board of *School Mental Health*.

About the authors

Professor Alan Dyson

Alan is Professor of Education in the University of Manchester, where he co-directs the Centre for Equity in Education and leads work on education in urban contexts. His research interests include the relationship between social and educational inclusion in urban contexts and, in particular, the relationship between education and other areas of public policy. Recent work include evaluations of the national extended ('full service') schools initiatives in England, a review of the research literature on schools and communities, and studies of the role of education in reducing health inequalities in England and in Europe. In 2001, he led the production of the Open File on Inclusive Education for UNESCO, and his recent books (with colleagues) include *Beyond the School Gates: Can Full Service and Extended Schools Overcome Disadvantage?* (Routledge, 2011), *Education and Poverty in Affluent Countries* (Routledge, 2010), and *Improving Schools, Developing Inclusion* (Routledge, 2006). Alan has worked in universities since 1988, before which he spent 13 years as a teacher, mainly in urban comprehensive schools.

Professor Peter Farrell

Peter is a Professor of Special Needs and Educational Psychology in the University of Manchester and former President of the International School Psychology Association. He has directed, or co-directed, a number of research projects for the Department for Education and other organizations, many of which have focused on inclusive education. These include projects on the role of teaching assistants, the inclusion of pupils with Down's syndrome, and the relationship between inclusion and pupil achievement in mainstream schools. He is the author of a number of books and articles on inclusive education and has been a keynote speaker on this topic at international conferences in several countries, including Hong Kong, Estonia, Malaysia, Australia, Greece, South Africa, and India.

Dr. Martin Hanbury

As a headmaster at a highly successful, specialist school for children with autism in the North-West of England, Martin brings a strong practitioner focus/voice to his contribution and to the book more generally. He is also an emerging scholar within the field of autism and an inspiring associate tutor for Edge Hill University working on the SEN/Inclusion pathway. Martin has written a successful and extremely useful educational publication about practice with children/young people who have autism.

Dr. Terry Hanley

Terry is joint Programme Director of the Doctorate in Counselling Psychology at the University of Manchester and an experienced youth counsellor. For his therapeutic practice he is registered in the UK by the Health Professions Council as a counselling psychologist and is a British Psychological Society chartered psychologist. He is an Associate Fellow of the British Psychological Society and the Research Lead for the Division of Counselling Psychology (DCoP). He has published widely in the field of youth counselling and is also the Editor of the DCoP's research publication *Counselling Psychology Review*.

Professor Neil Humphrey

Neil is Professor of Psychology of Education at the University of Manchester. His main research interests are social and emotional learning, mental health, and special educational needs. Neil has published extensively in these areas, authoring (or co-authoring) over 50 journal articles, book chapters, and research reports. He has led (or collaborated on) projects funded by the Department for Education, Economic and Social Research Council, Centre for Excellence in Outcomes, Joseph Rowntree Foundation, and the Association for Educational Psychologists.

Dr. Hazel Lawson

Hazel is a Senior Lecturer in Special and Inclusive Education at the University of Exeter. She was formerly a primary and special schoolteacher and has research interests in curriculum development and pupil involvement for children and young people with severe learning difficulties. She is fascinated by the exploration of methods and methodologies in researching people's perceptions and stories.

Dr. Clare Lennie

Clare is joint Programme Director of the Doctorate in Counselling Psychology at the University of Manchester. Before this she worked in the sixth-form setting for ten years as a psychology tutor and student counsellor, before moving into higher education and lecturing on teacher training programmes. She has a particular interest in counselling psychology in the prison setting and is registered in the UK by the Health Professions Council as a counselling psychologist and is a British Psychological Society chartered psychologist.

Carolyn Purslow

Carolyn is the Deputy Head at Ellen Tinkham School, Exeter, with responsibility for Transition, Post-14 curriculum development, and school-based research. Carolyn is a trained facilitator for person-centred reviews and a person-centred approach is embedded across the school community. She was the Lead Practitioner Coordinator for SEND with the Specialist Schools and Academies Trust for three years and in

2011 worked for the Complex Learning Difficulties and Disabilities (CLDD) Research Project focusing on personalized transition.

Dr. Barbara Riddick

Barbara is a scholar with an international reputation in considering notions of labelling around SEN and the experience of children with SpLDs/SEN. Her seminal publication, *Living with Dyslexia* (Routledge, 1996), has recently been updated and re-issued in its second edition (Routledge, 2010). Barbara is also a part-time active consultant psychologist working with children/young people for the NHS.

List of boxes, figures, and table

DAVID ARMSTRONG AND GARRY SQUIRES
Introduction

We asked the contributing authors to write in a controversial and thought-provoking style that is informed by their expertise yet encourages you, the reader, to come to your own conclusions. In editing this book, we have been heartened by the depth and breadth of contributions by our authors, surpassing even our high expectations. This level of commitment by authors is even more welcome given the complex and controversial history of special education and also in light of the current turbulence around special educational needs and disability (SEND) in the UK.

An uncertainty over the future pervades what follows but, more positively, it offers creative opportunities for new growth and progress that are richly embraced by the contributors. Such positive possibilities are also re-addressed in the book's conclusion, Chapter 9, which summarizes previous chapters through imagining an 'ideal' educational setting in light of previous chapters. At the end of Chapter 9, we invite you to construct your ideal school for meeting the needs of children with SEND. We hope that you enjoy this challenge and that the act of reflecting on the text – agreeing with some parts, disagreeing with other parts, debating the issues with other readers and colleagues – will help you to develop your professional practice whether you are a teacher, teaching assistant, school manager, psychologist or local authority officer.

Structure of the book

Structurally, this book is divided into two distinct but overlapping parts. Section 1 addresses some of the wide, and often pervasive, issues that cut across theory, practice, and policy around the education of children and young people with SEND: the historical agendas, and resulting tensions, currently affecting inclusion for children/ young people with forms of SEND (Chapter 1); issues around labelling of individuals with categories of SEND (Chapter 2); a critical view of debates around the prevalence of special schools (Chapter 3); and the wider influence of social processes on special education and concepts of inclusion (Chapter 4). The purpose of Section 1 is to offer you a thought-provoking overview of the context of education in this area, drawing out some of the wider and deeper issues inherent in everyday practice and in the dilemmas it can pose.

Section 2 extends this exploration by focusing on key discrete topics disclosed by educators, educationalists, and research in discussing practice, particularly in light of increased calls over the last 20 years that it should attend to the wider needs of the child or young person with SEND. The implications of this holistic view are addressed: in considering the role of mental health and of therapeutic interventions in the educational setting (Chapter 5); through an exploration of what concepts such as self-esteem imply for a child's learning and development (Chapter 6); via attention to the notion of students' participation in their learning and decisions made that affect them (Chapter 7); and in considering the issue of a child's behaviour as part of a wider set of relationships (Chapter 8).

The contribution of psychology as a discipline and of a wider psychological perspective on learning is evident – and very welcome – in this book. Chapter 5 (The therapeutic classroom) and Chapter 6 (Self-esteem in the classroom) in particular underscore the great value that psychology, as the systematic study of the human mind and of human behaviour, has for understanding how we differ and in how we are also (paradoxically) the same in our underlying thought processes and broad patterns of development. This wider, developmental perspective is of particular value for an informed educational practice with children described as facing a difficulty with their learning, and thereby perceived as having barriers to the 'typical' processes such as socialization or appropriate behaviour that support learning.

Overview of the story

The psychology of education is a well-established discipline drawing on developmental psychology, organizational psychology, interpersonal psychology, intrapersonal psychology, and related disciplines of sociology, anthropology, philosophy, politics, and educational pedagogy. Together with psychology, perspectives taken from political and social science strongly influence chapters within this book; indeed, we would suggest that the education of all children, but particularly those defined as 'different', is deeply, inescapably, political. The contributions here offer the reader an enriching psychologically informed framework on which to progress their own thought and consequent actions in practice. Chapter 5, for example, asks the reader to consider children who might be (mis)categorized as 'sad, bad or mad' and to consider possible therapeutic interventions that move beyond this, drawing out implications for educators; Chapter 6 is a thought-provoking and research-informed overview of the self-system in children and of many sub-terms used by teachers (and everybody else) such as 'self-esteem' in describing others. Particular implications for children with SEND are highlighted in an extended discussion of how the notion that they are 'special' can make them feel anything but special: this is an important area for current research.

The immense value of a historical perspective on what we currently describe as SEND is underlined by Garry Squires in Chapter 1. Educators, along with many other professionals, often suggest that their professional lives feel as though they are on a treadmill taking them briskly into an immediate future, without a chance to look back and reflect. A danger is that the here and now is an evolving consequence of the many events, actions (or lack of actions), perceptions, laws, and accidents that spring from the past but weigh on our current thought and action – often without our conscious awareness of their role in affecting our behaviour and perception. Chapter 1 offers (the important luxury of) an informed and critical overview of the history of special education, drawing out the tensions and implications for the (more recent) agenda of inclusion for children with SEND. As such, it provides a vital anchor for the book as a whole and a context for subsequent chapters – developing some of the wider themes presented in this introduction. The sheer elasticity of SEND as a descriptive category is, in particular, made evident by Chapter 1.

Chapter 2 focuses this insight, exploring what it means to label children with forms of SEND (dyslexia is used as an example of the case in point). This highly sensitive and hugely important issue for educational practice/policy is expertly handled, referring to Barbara Riddick's own seminal research in this area (see references at the end of this book). Chapter 2 makes this complex topic accessible by drawing our attention to the wide range of psychological reactions that labelling provokes. Of great value for any reader is the guidance (or protocol) that Barbara Riddick offers in the forms of reflective questions and as a guide to labelling wisely. This will, we predict, be immensely useful to any educator: offering them the core of a more considered and nuanced approach to children and young people.

One of the most important practical consequences of labelling for children or young people is how this often influences where they are subsequently educated. Many families of children with SEND and children/young people themselves attest to the profound impact that placement in specialist provision, rather than mainstream education, or vice versa, can have on a child's subsequent development, academic attainment, and view of themselves.

Chapter 3, by Peter Farrell, outlines the important relationship between the continued existence of special schools in the UK and notions of inclusion as understood by successive governments in the UK. In an extremely thought-provoking analysis, he concludes that there has been no change in the number of children placed in special schools over the last 20 years and that, under certain influential definitions of inclusion, no appreciable progress has therefore been made. He argues that a clear commitment to inclusion by politicians is now vital – particularly in light of the apparent message in the Green Paper (DfE, 2011b) that, in his words, 'inclusion has gone far enough'. Peter's principled and highly informed analysis notes the distorting influence of self-interested rhetoric by politicians: in order to argue against inclusion, the view of the public is managed to create the impression that (scandalously) specialist provision was now, in the UK, almost nil. Readers who are familiar with political science, social science or critical accounts of the role of the contemporary media might recognize such strategies to control the landscape of debate.

Chapter 4, by Alan Dyson, suggests that disadvantaging factors in students' backgrounds have often been neglected or underplayed and that these factors lead to many of these children underachieving. He draws attention to how this shortcoming has limited the success of educational interventions, often resulting in an asocial focus on a child's individual difficulties. There have been positive efforts in the UK over the last fifteen years to try to address these social inequalities. He argues that special needs education should be part of a much wider strategy for tackling the connections between social and educational disadvantage. In making these arguments, Alan explores a hidden issue and what many educators realize at an implicit level: that poverty, family background, and social inequality are often pervasive contextual factors in the lives of children who have SEND. Chapter 4 offers a radical and holistic response to this controversial topic.

This explicitly political agenda to the education of children with SEND is approached from a positive, yet critically realistic perspective by Hazel Lawson and Carolyn Purslow in Chapter 7: the democratic classroom. As they suggest, in this context, notions of democracy have been recently enacted in the UK, USA, and Australasia via the promotion of student voice, pupil participation, renovated teacher–student relationships, cooperative learning, and citizenship programmes. They highlight the potential problems, and potential benefits, of a democratized classroom for young people with SEND, offering case studies of how this might operate in practice. An important conclusion reached is that principled, ethical relationships between learner and educator are vital for progress. They also indicate that honesty, reflection, and realism are key qualities for professionals working within the institutional constraints that often work against democratic values. An important suggestion made, in light of this analysis, is the need for wider cultural change within education, starting with current perceptions of children and young people. It is significant that other chapters within this publication reach the same conclusion: that to move forward in practice involves, at the very least, honest scrutiny of the values, perceptions, systems, and habits that we and colleagues hold – and may consider core to our professional/personal identity.

The behaviour of children and young people in educational settings is an issue that can consistently challenge an educator's professional identity, provoking self-reflection, personal anxiety, and raising unsettling questions. On a wider level, in the UK and elsewhere, this topic elicits a disparate set of reactions from educational leaders, the media, politicians, and policy-shapers. Some public reaction about the behaviour of children and young people is thoughtful; on occasion comments in the public domain are dismally uniformed. Too often such debates are unhelpful for teachers, the children affected, and their families, insofar as they do not offer insights that are applicable for everyday practice in the classroom.

In Chapter 8, Martin Hanbury suggests that, in the context of learning, it is beneficial to stress human relationships rather than behaviour. He succinctly identifies the value of reconsidering behaviour in this way and outlines a holistic ethical framework within which facets of learning can be systematically addressed for children or young people with SEND. Martin's account offers a rich, realistic, account of how a focus on developing positive relationships can enhance the learning and larger lives of children, offering them deeply important transferable skills. A unique quality of this chapter is its reference to the wider organizational implications of a cultural shift towards developing positive relationships (and away from emphasizing behaviour). Here Martin's own role as a seasoned practitioner and head of a very successful school for children with autism shines through. Chapter 8 is candid about the challenges inherent in making meaningful change around behaviour and at an institutional level but it offers hope. In common with the positive emphasis of other chapters, Martin underscores how success with often vulnerable children promises real innovation in pedagogy to the benefit of all learners.

In Chapter 9, David Armstrong reflects on the contributions of the different authors and imaginatively creates an ideal school. He teases the reader with a vision of 'what might be', if only we have the will and political impetus to turn the vision into reality. He daringly asks how far you, the readers, are prepared to put some of the ideas contained in this book into practice. In case you do not like David's view of an ideal school, he invites you to create your own vision at the end of the chapter.

What follows is therefore richly informed by perspectives from politics, sociology, and psychology but its most important quality, in unsettled times, is in suggesting paths towards more stable future ground.

SECTION 1

In this section, the contributing authors introduce some of the wide, and often pervasive, issues that cut across theory, practice, and policy around the education of children and young people with special educational needs and disability (SEND).

Chapter 1 covers the historical, political and social agendas, and resulting tensions, currently affecting inclusion for children/young people with forms of SEND. Chapter 2 explores issues around labelling of individuals with categories of SEND. Chapter 3 takes a critical view of debates around the prevalence of special schools. Chapter 4 looks at the wider influence of social processes on special education and concepts of inclusion.

The purpose of Section 1 is to offer you a thought-provoking overview of the context of education in this area, drawing out some of the wider and deeper issues inherent in everyday practice and in the dilemmas it can pose.

1

GARRY SQUIRES
Historical and socio-political agendas around defining and including children with special educational needs

Most children/young people in the UK have a happy and effective education and go onto become well-adjusted and successful adults. This is important to say, in the face of what might be called 'moral panics' about the state of education, behaviour of young people or competency of teachers.

Teachers and teaching assistants genuinely want to do the best for their pupils. They are hardworking and dedicated professionals. But what does 'best' mean and is it the same for everyone? How does this lead to some schools managing some pupils better than others with better outcomes (and which outcomes)? There are many agendas and political tensions facing teachers and schools that can make it more likely or less likely that they can support and include pupils with special educational needs. Where did these agendas come from? What value systems underpin them? What practices do these lead educators to engage in? How can reflecting on them help the educational professional think about the kind of classroom in which they would want to work to support the whole child with special educational needs? This book will help the reader to explore these issues using topics chosen to illustrate some of the questions outlined here. The contributing authors come from a variety of educational perspectives and have been asked to write in a controversial way and a way that brings out some of the tensions. And, of course, they will have a view based on their own value systems that may or may not coincide with that of the reader. We hope that this will make you reflect on your own perspective. As you read the book, there may be moments when the different agendas seem to pull in opposing directions and you are left feeling confused – this is good; you now have permission to decide where you stand.

Historical influences on the inclusion of children with special needs in England and Wales

When we consider the notion of universal education and the vision of the developments in international thinking about inclusion, it is hard to imagine how much has changed in UK education. The Salamanca Agreement set out the expectation of promoting 'the approach of inclusive education, namely enabling schools to serve all children, particularly those with special educational needs' (UNESCO, 1994b, p. 3).

The Dakar Agreement extended this aim and set out a number of challenges to improve inclusive education worldwide by 2015 with 'total inclusion of children with special needs in the mainstream schools' (UNESCO, 2000, p. 71). However, the historical and political path taken to arrive at this point has been long and many of the arguments and tensions created along the way continue to influence current educational practice. This leads to a gap between the vision and policy and another gap between policy and practice. It means that there is much variation on the ground, between local authorities, between schools, and even between classrooms in the same school. In this section, we present a brief overview of the history of special educational needs and disability (SEND) to draw out some of the tensions. We invite, you the reader, to consider how this historical context contributes to your view about inclusion and the views of your colleagues. To what extent do the different ways of viewing special educational needs impact on your daily practice and in what ways does this help or hinder what you are hoping to achieve?

Prior to the nineteenth century, only a small proportion of children went to school. This was changed by the 1870 Education Act and subsequent 1880 Education Act leading to compulsory education for all children between the age of 5 and 10 years. Fees were abolished in 1891 and the age of compulsory schooling extended to 12 years by 1899. Within this context there was a notion that some children might not be able to benefit from the limited curriculum offered in local schools. Some children with particular difficulties were not offered compulsory state education until the establishment of special schools for blind and deaf children in 1893, followed by special schools for physically impaired children (referred to as 'defective and epileptic children') in 1899 (Living Heritage, 2010).

From 1862 to 1897, teachers depended on good examination results to ensure that their school received appropriate funding under a system commonly referred to as 'Payment by Results'. If children did not achieve an acceptable standard in reading, writing, and arithmetic, money was withheld (Rapple, 1994). Consequently, if teachers wished to receive a good salary, they had to develop effective strategies for maximizing the return on their effort. There was a danger that some teachers would concentrate on those children that they saw as profitable and ignore those that they thought would not reach the required standard. Bright children would reach the required standard easily, they required less attention from the teacher, and did not always receive the challenge that they needed to keep them engaged and maximize their learning. Academically weaker children were seen as hindering the progress of other children in large over-crowded classes. Those children who just failed to meet the required standard received most of the teacher's attention. Market forces also dictated where teachers would take their skills. Teachers chose schools that they thought would have a greater percentage of pupil passes to increase the likelihood of them receiving a good salary. Managers selected those teachers whom they thought would bring about the best results. The economic pressures meant that 'good schools' got better at ensuring that good pupils got good teachers. In some schools, 'dull pupils' were refused admittance. There was also growing concern about 'maladjusted children' who had emotional and behavioural difficulties and were disrupting lessons and preventing other children from learning.

Similar events were happening in other countries. The French government was concerned about children who would not benefit from the mainstream education on offer. They wanted to differentiate between those children who could learn but chose not to ('the malicious') and those who could not learn at the same rate as their peers (Howe, 1997; Thorndike, 1997). The Minister for Public Instruction wanted a way of identifying children who were 'mentally subnormal' and wanted an indication of the degree of subnormality. This led to a test being developed and published in 1905 by Alfred Binet and Theodore Simon that allowed children to be classified according to their mental age (Wasserman & Tulsky, 2005). This allowed political decisions to be made about whether a child would be offered an educational placement in a mainstream school or not. Further refinements in the test by Lewis Terman at Stanford University and by Stern in 1912 led to the development of the concept of an intelligence quotient. This quickly led to the notion that children could be screened to determine whether they were bright enough to benefit from the teaching on offer and political decisions made at a local level by local councils. In the USA, a new tension was created – that between placing children in classes according to their chronological age or placing them in classes according to their mental age. Children no longer progressed with their age-related peers but could be held back until they were ready for the next class (now referred to as a 'grade retention' in many countries or 'over-age retention' in the UK).

In 40 years, the education system in the UK had already produced complexity and gaps between vision and practice. There was an idealized view that all children should be educated in their local neighbourhood mainstream schools. Yet policy had developed that allowed some children to be excluded from mainstream schools and educated in special schools on the basis of certain medical conditions. The 1902 Education Act allowed local councils to develop a local policy on education to meet local needs (taking a lead from the government's Board of Education, whose role remained to control education in England and Wales). A mechanism for testing children's cognitive ability and likelihood of benefiting from the education on offer had been devised. Local practice had led to some schools barring admission to some groups of pupils. Within schools, further decisions were made about educational progression and over-age retention.

Formal testing procedures were being developed to aid political decisions to be made locally by district councils. The councils needed to have a basis for making decisions and turned to medical officers to provide professional advice about who would go to mainstream schools, who would go to special schools, and which children would not receive any education on the grounds that they were 'ineducable'. The difficulty was that medical officers had not received any psychological training and were finding it difficult to make decisions about pupils with low IQ or with emotional and behavioural difficulties. The London County Council employed its first educational psychologist, Cyril Burt, to help solve this problem of classifying children's suitability for schooling (Squires & Farrell, 2006). Towards the end of the 1920s, this had spread across many other local authorities and there was a move towards multi-professional assessment at Child Guidance Centres. A team consisting of a psychiatrist, psychologist, physician, and social worker met together to make educational placement decisions and were additionally tasked with trying to understand and prevent juvenile misbehaviour.

The 1944 Butler Education Act required local authorities to provide education for children who were 'subnormal', maladjusted or physically handicapped. It also introduced compulsory education at secondary level with a school leaving age of

15 years. Secondary aged children were divided into three groups, who received different types of mainstream education depending on whether they attended grammar schools (for the academically elite), secondary technical schools (though not many were ever produced) or secondary modern schools (for the majority of pupils). Children were allocated places at one of the school types on the basis of their results in an examination called the '11 plus', with the top 25 per cent of pupils going to the grammar schools. The notion of a specialist education system for those pupils who did not fit in with the schooling offered to the majority continued. The 1944 Act considered some children to have a 'disability of mind or body' that required a different type of education (HMSO, 1944, see section 34). It reinforced the medical model of some children having problems that fitted neatly into one of eleven categories of 'handicap' that could be 'diagnosed' and required specialist 'treatment'. These categories were detailed in *The Handicapped Pupils and School Health Service Regulations 1945* (Ministry of Education, 1945):

- blind
- partially sighted
- deaf
- partially deaf
- delicate
- diabetic
- educationally subnormal
- epileptic
- maladjusted
- physically handicapped
- speech defects.

Those children who were deemed ineducable became the responsibility of the Department of Health and Social Services and were not entitled to receive statutory education. The 1944 Act produced further categorization of types of pupil and an increasingly diverse education system to deal with the different categories produced. The tendency was towards segregated education rather than towards universal inclusivity. However, this last requirement led to a definition of special educational needs that has had a lasting impact and was repeated in government policy documents and Education Acts for the next 60 years (see Box 1.1).

Box 1.1 Defining special educational needs (see, for example, HMSO, 1981)

'A child has a 'learning difficulty' for the purposes of this Act if –

(a) he has a significantly greater difficulty in learning than the majority of children of his age,

(b) he has a disability which either prevents or hinders him from making use of educational facilities of a kind generally provided for children of his age in schools within the area of the local education authority, or

(c) he is under compulsory school age and is, or would be if special educational provision were not made for him, likely to fall within paragraph (a) or (b) when of that age.

In this Act 'special educational provision' means –

(a) in relation to a child who has attained the age of two, educational provision which is additional to, or otherwise different from, the educational provision made generally for children of his age in schools maintained by the local education authority (other than special schools) and

(b) in relation to a child under that age, educational provision of any kind.'

Note: Text taken from the Education Acts 1981 and 1996.

The Minister for Education had increasing concerns about the education of maladjusted children and in 1950 set up the Underwood Committee to look at the training for teachers to improve their treatment. The Committee reported in 1955. One of the main contributions was to reject the previous medical definitions of 'maladjustment' that tended to focus on psychiatric disturbance and emotional instability, to a definition that took a more social-environmental perspective and widened the range of children to include introverted and withdrawn children under the label:

> . . . a child may be regarded as maladjusted who is developing in ways that have a bad effect on himself or his fellows, and cannot without help be remedied by his parents, teachers and other adults ordinarily in contact with him.
>
> (Underwood Report, 1955, p. 22)

Some authors believe that the move towards a social-educational definition of 'maladjustment' meant that the term became a catch-all for many different types of emotional and behavioural difficulty, such as delinquency, mental illness, and social deprivation (Laslett, 1998; Visser, 2003). However, the medical model prevailed, partly because a diagnosis of maladjustment was made by medical practitioners who were concerned with 'symptoms' and 'treatment'. The National Union for Teachers picked up on teachers' concerns about their role in working with children who had a medical condition by redefining the term further to include children who might be 'mildly difficult' (NUT, 1962).

A shift in thinking was brought about in 1978 with the publication of the Warnock Report (Warnock, 1978). The report stated that children should be educated in mainstream schools wherever this was possible and emphasized inclusion and integration rather than segregated provision. It cited 1.8 per cent of children at that time attending special schools, but with massive variation – for example, one London borough had ten times as many 'maladjusted' children in special provision than its neighbouring borough. The report also defined the population of children with special educational needs (SEN) as being one in five pupils. This figure is often quoted but the report went on to say that these pupils would have difficulty at some point in their schooling, but it was unlikely to be a long-term disability or disorder (Warnock, 1978, section 3.19). The categories of handicap introduced by the 1944 Act were called into question, particularly regarding the social stigma attached to such labels as 'educationally subnormal (moderate)' or 'maladjusted'. The committee called for the abolition of the use of categories for defining SEN. The Warnock Report commented on the rising numbers of pupils with learning difficulties that were being placed in special rather than in mainstream schools. The reported numbers had risen from 12,060 in 1947 to 22,639 in 1955 (with another 27,000 waiting placement).

The Warnock Report led to the 1981 Education Act, which introduced Statements of Special Educational Need intended for those children with the most complex and severe needs (HMSO, 1981). The Act made the teacher responsible for identifying and providing for special educational needs (section 5c). Yet at the same time, it required local authorities to be responsible for assessment and placement and ensuring that educational needs were met. For children who were assessed and a Statement of SEN written, it was the local authority that was responsible for providing additional resources to schools to meet the child's needs. This introduced a tension between local authorities and schools. Teachers considered that there were more children who needed to be assessed and local authorities were concerned about the expenditure that this would involve and the need to protect the public purse. The 1981 Act also gave parents the right to appeal to their local authority against the content of the Statement.

The 1988 Education Reform Act was aimed at driving up standards in education. It was not specifically about special educational needs but it had implications for the teaching of children with SEN. Specifically, it introduced a National Curriculum that was intended to be followed by all children, irrespective of ability or placement. Children in special schools would follow the curriculum, albeit at a lower level than children in mainstream schools. Potentially, this meant that transfer between special school and mainstream school was easier as the same curriculum was being followed.

One of the concerns before the National Curriculum had been the underperformance of girls and the curriculum was designed to take this into account and to spread assessment across the key stages rather than relying on summative assessments and single examinations (Burman, 2005). Over time this led to girls' academic performance outstripping that of boys. It is clear that more boys than girls are categorized as having special educational needs. Figures for Wales in 2008 revealed that 70 per cent of children with SEN were boys; boys were nine times more likely to have a diagnosis of autism and four times more likely to be labelled as having emotional and behavioural difficulties (Estyn, 2008). Together with the rising ratio of female to male teachers in the classroom, this has led to a popular view that differences in performance between the sexes were the result of the feminization of education (Parkin, 2007). This view, however, is not supported by research evidence. Teachers' gender has been shown not to have an effect on attainment in the Netherlands (Driessen, 2007), or to affect the outcome of remedial programmes for reading (Martin & Rezai-Rashti, 2009).

The 1988 Act also applied Keynesian economics supply–demand concepts through the introduction of quasi-market forces in education, where parents were given the freedom to choose the schools that they wanted and thus drive up demand for 'good schools' at the expense of 'underperforming schools'. Measures of perform-ance were introduced via the National Curriculum with a common set of examinations for all pupils at set stages of their schooling through Key Stage Standard Attainment Tests (SATs). Open enrolment to schools was accompanied with the publication of school performance tables (referred to as league tables) so that parents would be informed about school performance and could make choices about which school to send their children. With local management of finances freeing schools from local authority budgetary control, this meant that schools had to compete with each other. Parents were more likely to want to send their children to schools that performed well in league tables and this meant that head teachers wanted their school to do well on measures of SAT performance. Consequently, pupils with SEND who would not perform well on SATs were seen as less favourable and the unintended consequence of the Act was a return to the 'Payments by Results' scenario for children with SEN. At the same time, the inspection regime for ensuring good-quality teaching shifted away from local authorities (who knew their schools well) and Her Majesty's Inspectors to Ofsted (a more distant and supposedly objective means of inspection). This created new threats for teachers who saw the Ofsted inspections as a means of judging their individual performances and they became less tolerant of pupils with emotional and behavioural difficulties who might disrupt their lessons while an Ofsted inspector was in the classroom. These unintended consequences of the 1988 Act remain: forces that act against inclusion and either create demand for additional support for pupils with SEN from local authorities, or create demand for alternative placements. Before the 1988 Act, there had been a gradual reduction in the special school population but the 1988 Act brought an end to this trend. The Audit Commission reported almost the same number of children were being educated in special schools in 2002 as had been since the introduction of local management of schools (Audit Commission, 2002). Over the last four years, there has been a steady decline in mainstream education for children with statements (from 123,570 in 2006 to 105,190 in 2009) and an increase in special school placement over the same period (Ofsted, 2010).

Inclusion continued to be emphasized in the 1993 Education Act and its associ-ated Code of Practice for SEN. The act strengthened parents' right of appeal against local authority decisions through the establishment of the SEN Tribunal system. The number of appeals made by parents against local authority decisions increased year on year from 1161 in 1994 to a peak of 3726 in 2005 before starting to decline to around 3000 in 2008 (SENDIST, 2003; Tribunals Service, 2009). The Act also introduced a staged approach to assessment. This required schools to demonstrate that they had been working with a child to try to address their learning difficulties before a statement would be produced. In 1997, the publication of *Excellence for All Children* moved the inclusion agenda on again by giving government support to the

Salamanca Agreement and setting out the progressive expansion of the capacity of mainstream schools to meet the needs of all pupils (DfEE, 1997).

The Special Educational Needs and Disability Act 2001 gave parents greater rights in challenging schools and local authorities to ensure that children with SEN were not discriminated against (HMSO, 2001). Further refinements to the SEN procedures were made in the 2001 Education Act and Code of Practice for Special Educational Needs (DfES, 2001b). This introduced the notion of teachers 'noticing' children's difficulties and 'adjusting' their teaching, increasing class teachers' responsibilities for meeting the educational needs of children in their care. The five stages of the previous Act were replaced with three levels of support:

- *School Action* – this is support that starts with the class teacher taking responsibility for teaching all of the children in her class. When children fail to make adequate progress, she can draw on additional advice and support from the school's Special Educational Needs Coordinator (SENCo).

- *School Action Plus* – when the school continues to have difficulty helping a child make adequate progress, it can call on outside specialists. There is a wide range of potential specialists who can support through assessment, intervention or ideas for the teacher to work differently with the child to include them in the classroom activities. It might involve specialist teachers from the local authority, educational welfare officers, educational psychologists, social workers or specialists from the health authority, such as speech and language therapists, clinical psychologists, and paediatricians.

- *Statement of SEN* – this follows a multi-professional assessment commissioned by the local authority and building on the assessments undertaken at School Action and School Action Plus to provide an assessment over time.

This all sounds very well in principle, but the definition of what is meant by 'adequate progress' outlined in the Code of Practice is very inclusive, having different levels of meaning depending on the severity of need of the child. In practice, teachers and parents often refer to the meaning that implies 'catching up with peers'. Together with the expectation that most pupils will achieve a certain level of attainment at the end of the Key Stage SATs, this creates a pressure to move through the different levels quickly and to make requests of the local authority for statutory assessment, so that additional resources will become available to the school. The school then uses additional money to buy teaching assistant time either to support the child in class or to run intervention programmes. Over time, this has led to many teachers becoming deskilled in meeting the needs of children through differentiation or adaptation of their teaching. Consequently, there is a pressure from teachers to ask for teaching assistant time to support children with SEN in their classroom – often citing the needs of the rest of the learners in the class. In addition, head teachers want to maintain any additional support possible to class teachers through the employment of teaching assistants. With pressures on school budgets, SENCos are often asked to put more children forward for statutory assessment. The children targeted tend to be those that would be assessed quickly and meet easily defined criteria rather than the most needy pupils. This led to what has been termed a perverse incentive – schools having to show that teaching had failed to secure more funding through this method rather than attempting to improve teaching across the school to ensure that fewer children failed. The system as it stood was one that worked against inclusion by placing too much emphasis on statutory assessment to build up an army of teaching assistants to deal with a swelling number of children defined as having moderate learning difficulties. The number of teaching assistants had risen from 64,200 in 1997 to 103,600 in 2002 and to 181,600 in 2009 (DCSF, 2009; DfES, 2002). There were almost three times as many teaching assistants in 2009 as there were in 1997. Often teachers do not have time set aside to allow them to coordinate, plan jointly or share monitoring information with teaching assistants (Blatchford et al., 2009b). There were concerns that teaching assistant training was patchy and this limited teaching assistants' impact on children's progress and inclusion (Cajkler et al., 2007). A more recent study suggests that the more support children get, the less academic progress they make (Blatchford et al., 2009a; Webster et al., 2010). A systematic literature review found that teaching assistants do have a positive effect when their support is targeted through well-structured interventions in literacy and language. However, when they were not used in a targeted or systematic way (e.g. providing *ad hoc* support in the classroom), no difference was evident (Farrell, Alborz, Howes, & Pearson, 2010).

The wording in the Code of Practice continued to move away from a medical model of assessment by emphasizing teaching and learning and the child's development in key areas. The guidance makes no assumptions about 'hard and fast categories of special educational need' (DfES, 2001b, p. 85), and instead promoted the consideration of need across four broad areas:

- communication and interaction
- cognition and learning
- behavioural, emotional, and social development
- sensory and/or physical.

The move away from the medical model turned attention towards educational interventions that started with the class teacher and did not rely on costly assessment to be able to provide an intervention. However, central government has continued to monitor SEN across a number of categories that are in tension to this notion and that continue to reinforce a medical model. These categories are still a feature of the Pupil Level Census data:

- autistic spectrum disorder
- physical disability
- multi-sensory impairment
- visual impairment
- hearing impairment
- speech, language, and communication difficulty
- behavioural, emotional, and social difficulty

- profound and multiple learning difficulty
- severe learning difficulty
- moderate learning difficulty
- specific learning difficulty
- other learning difficulty/disability.

A quasi-medical model remains for young people over the age of 16 who are defined using terms introduced in the Disability Discrimination Act 1995 (HMSO, 1995). Learning difficulties and/or disabilities (LDD) refers to either a significant difficulty in learning compared with the majority of people of that age in post-16 education or training, or to a physical or mental impairment that is substantial and likely to interfere with normal day-to-day activities. The term 'diagnosis' continues to permeate education-alists and can be found in the most recent Ofsted review of SEND (Ofsted, 2010).

The Audit Commission looked at the rising trend in the number of Statements produced (Audit Commission, 2002). In 2001–2002, 15 per cent of the schools budget was spent on SEN. The majority of pupils with SEN (34 per cent) were identified as having moderate learning difficulties. Sixty-one per cent of children with Statements were educated in mainstream schools. The number of Statements reaches a peak when children transfer to secondary school. Exclusions for children with SEN in special schools were higher than for children in mainstream schools and attendance was lower. Most exclusions in mainstream schools were for children with SEN, suggesting that their educational needs were not being addressed with the level of support that they were receiving. The cost of providing a Statement often outweighed the benefit the Statement provided. A number of recommendations emerged, including:

- *Changing funding arrangements.* Many local authorities responded to this by devolving money that was being held back to provide additional support via the Statement. This meant that schools had the money in their budgets to respond flexibly to the needs of children without having to go through the statutory assessment process. Statements were still issued but these did not carry any additional resources. One of the changes that this led to was a reduction in requests for statutory assessment, with local authority support service time prioritized to deal with more complex and needy pupils who often required extended involvement to help teachers meet their needs in mainstream settings.

- *Extending the role of special schools to provide advice to mainstream schools.* Many authorities found ways of allocating money to allow this to happen and to develop outreach roles for special schools. The hope was that this would lead to increased capacity in mainstream schools and lead to a reduction in special school places. In practice, the teachers from special schools often spotted a child in the mainstream that their mainstream colleagues were struggling with and suggested that the child should transfer to the special school.

- *SENCos should be more informed about the funding available in their school* for SEN and able to evaluate how the funding was used and the benefits derived for children with SEN. This aim led to the Audit Commission developing its Value for Money toolkit for Special Educational Needs (Audit Commission, 2008).

- *More time should be made available to SENCos to fulfil their role.* The majority of SENCos were expected to spend too much time teaching and did not have sufficient time to coordinate special educational needs effectively in their school. However, there was no additional funding to schools to allow SENCos to have reduced teaching loads and to be released to meet with parents, outside specialists or work support teachers and teaching assistants. This remains a challenge today.

The changing impact of league tables

The 1988 Act attempted to drive up education standards by setting out the conditions in which schools would compete with each other, and this competition was enhanced through the publication of school performance tables ('league tables'). The original league tables set out the number of pupils who were reaching the expected level of attainment in each school as a percentage score. This allowed a quick comparison of school performance. It did not take into account the relative intake of the pupils. If a school had a lot of pupils who entered school with low levels of development and progressed at the same rate as average children, they would still be below the expected level by the end of Key Stage 2. Many children starting school had not reached their expected developmental level for many reasons and would catch up within a few terms (examples include poor socio-economic status that could lead to missed learning opportunities; delays in language; and lack of pre-school nursery experience). This might have put pressure on head teachers to deny access to school by any pre-school children who might not be at the appropriate developmental level on entry to school. This could happen in quite different ways. For example, heads might say to a parent that the school down the road was very good at meeting their child's needs. Alternatively, they might exaggerate the school's inability to meet the child's needs and suggest that a special school placement might be more appropriate and advise the parent to ask the local authority to undertake statutory assessment.

Value added measures were introduced to school performance tables to try to make comparison between schools easier and to take into account differences in starting points. At first glance this appeared to deal with those children who started school with lower developmental levels than their peers and seemed to reduce the pressure on head teachers to suggest that the children's needs would be better met elsewhere. Value added can be thought about in its simplest form as taking the national average of all pupils' attainments at a previous key stage and comparing with to their current attainments. An individual pupil's progress can then be compared with the average progress. A school can be scored based on the average value added scores of all of its pupils. This is regardless of individual pupil characteristics or circumstances. Children with SEN would be expected to make less progress than 'average' children and would consequently lower the overall score for the school and make them less desirable to managers in mainstream education. The pressure remained for head teachers to persuade parents that their child needed to be educated in a special school so that they would no longer be on the school's roll. This could happen at two key points – either before entry (to prevent them ever appearing on the school roll) or before completing Key Stage 2 (to prevent them appearing on the statistical returns and being included in the league tables). Many head teachers were happy for children to start in their school but then moved them quickly through the assessment processes so that they would receive a Statement and a possible alternative placement.

In January 2004, the government started to address this concern and changed the way that value added was to be calculated. David Miliband set out the principle of 'context value added', which 'adjusts predicted achievement to take account of not only prior attainment, but also a range of other factors observed to impact on performance which are outside a school's control' (DfES, 2006c).

Further refinements continue to be made. In 2009, the Department for Children, Schools and Families and Ofsted jointly published a document outlining plans to replace league tables with a school report card, which was intended to be introduced in the summer of 2011. The major benefits of the report card are:

> . . . that fair comparisons can be made between the performance of schools with different intakes and challenges. This is vital so that all schools, regardless of background or intake, have the same opportunity to perform well.
>
> (DCSF/Ofsted, 2009, p. 3)

The report card meant that schools would be graded on a number of factors including overall pupil attainment. They would be able to show simply whether this was improving, remaining steady or falling compared with the previous year. This reduces the pressure on schools not to include pupils who will not meet the national expectations at the end of Key Stage 2 and Key Stage 4, while still maintaining a pressure to drive up standards. One of the scores to be indicated on the proposed report card was the extent to which the school was able to 'narrow the gap' for pupils with SEN. The report card was to make use of contextual value added to take into account comparison with similar schools ('statistical neighbours' or 'families of schools') rather than neighbouring schools with different contextual factors. An approach considered for dealing with the reporting of pupils with SEN was to separate out their scores, but this was felt to be an incentive to schools to over-report the number of pupils with SEN. However, many head teachers already believe that identifying more children as having SEN will have a positive influence on the school's contextual value added score (Ofsted, 2010).

Further strategies and initiatives to promote inclusive practice in mainstream education

Standards in literacy dominated government thinking with the introduction of National Strategies in 1998 and the reworking of the teaching of literacy through the National Literacy Strategy. This set out the aspiration that 80 per cent of 11-year-old children would be able to perform at Level 4 of SATs or above by 2002 (DfEE, 1998). Whole-class teaching was seen as being important for all children including those with SEN. The actual numbers of pupils achieving these political targets was a lot less. In 1999, 75 per cent of boys and 82 per cent of girls reached the expected standard in reading; overall performance in writing stood at just over 50 per cent. By 2010, the number of pupils achieving the expected standard had risen but writing still lagged behind the aspiration and there remained a difference between boys and girls: 78 per cent of girls reached the expected standard compared with just 63 per cent of boys (DfE, 2010d). This has two effects on parents and teachers. First, any child who is not reaching the required standard can be perceived as not making adequate progress and defined as having SEN. Second, support is targeted to those children who just miss the political targets rather than to those children who have more severe or complex needs. Further refinements to the delivery of the curriculum followed to deal with those children who just missed the aspirational targets, including the intro-duction of special booster classes aimed at small groups of children. The belief was that intervention could enable these children to catch up to the expected standard.

More refinements followed with the concept of 'waves of support'. This built on the idea that whole-school teaching was best for most children and more targeted support was needed for some. The concept of quality first teaching meant that teachers had to think about all of the children in their class and consider best practice for teaching the class. Wave 1 intervention meant teachers noticing those children who did not cope with the original plan and adjusting their teaching through differ-entiation (e.g. different outcomes, different activities, different levels of support). Wave 2 was envisaged as small group work, such as ELS, ALS, FLS, and Springboard:

- Early Literacy Support (ELS) programme
- Additional Literacy Support (ALS) programme
- Further Literacy Support (FLS) programme
- Springboard (numeracy) programme.

It could also include other small group work such as speech and language therapy programmes or physiotherapy programmes. Wave 3 was seen as applying to a few children in each class and required more individual support, possibly with the guid-ance of outside specialists or following on from a statutory assessment.

Teachers' concern that they did not have sufficient knowledge or skills was addressed through the publication of guidance documents to support the literacy and numeracy curricula. This led to the Inclusion Development Programme, which is an online continuing professional development (CPD) programme that schools can use as part of the school development plan or individual teachers can select units to follow at their own pace. At the time of writing, the units available are:

- Dyslexia, introduced in 2008
- Speech and language and communication needs, introduced in 2008
- Supporting children on the autistic spectrum, introduced in 2009
- Supporting children on the autistic spectrum, early years foundation stage, introduced in 2009
- Supporting children with emotional and behavioural difficulties, introduced in 2010.

Further advice and reports were commissioned by the government to promote the political agenda of social inclusion. Examples include the report for identifying and teaching children with dyslexia (Rose, 2009); improving the identification of speech and language difficulties and a greater emphasis on teaching these skills in the primary curriculum (Bercow, 2008); the need for greater parental involvement and a stronger emphasis on SEN in schools (Lamb, 2009); a review of the availability of teachers for pupils with severe, profound, and multiple learning difficulties (Salt, 2010). Common themes that arise from these documents include:

- The need for early assessment and intervention
- Joint working across professional boundaries and easier access to services (building on the *Every Child Matters* agenda (DfES, 2004a))
- Services that are configured around families
- Improved communication with parents and the need to build parental confidence in the system and services provided
- The need to continue training all staff involved in educating children, especially those children and young people with the most complex needs.

Pilots to improve teaching and learning, the monitoring of SEN, and engagement with parents were introduced with Making Good Progress (2007–2009) and Achievement for All (2009–2011). Mental health and social well-being were targeted through the widespread introduction of the Social and Emotional Aspects for Learning and the Targeted Mental Health in Schools projects (DCSF, 2005, 2008c, 2008d, 2010; DfES, 2007). In parallel, the Child and Adolescent Mental Health Service was tasked with improving the knowledge and training of all adults who work with children through the development and delivery of Tier 1 training (Aggett, Boyd, & Fletcher, 2006; DCSF/DH, 2008, 2009; Health Advisory Service, 1995; NICE, 2008; Pettitt, 2003).

However, with the change of government following the 2010 elections there was a shift in educational policy. The Green Paper consulting on SEND introduces the phrase, 'remove the bias towards inclusion' (DfE, 2011b, pp. 5, 17, and 51). This emphasizes parental choice for special schools over mainstream schools and is discussed further by Farrell in Chapter 3.

Conclusions

In this chapter, I have discussed some of the historical influences on how children with SEND are defined and what enables or hinders their inclusion in mainstream education. Legislation has played a role in this process, by both promoting inclusion and also creating drivers that act against it. Although policy and educational context have changed, the definition of SEND remains the same as it was in 1944. There was a recognition that the way in which SEND was defined depended both on individual needs and on context. A child might be defined as having special educational needs in one school but not in another (DfEE, 1997).

Nationally, 1.5 million children were identified as having special educational needs in 1997 and this number remained steady until 2006 (DfE, 2010b; DfEE, 1997). In 2010, 1.7 million pupils were identified as having special educational needs (DfE, 2010b). This represents an overall increase of 2 per cent of the population between 2006 and 2010. The increase is mainly at School Action and School Action Plus with a slight drop in the number of pupils with Statements. Around 60 per cent of pupils with Statements attend mainstream schools. The majority of pupils with SEND were identified as having moderate learning difficulties and the next highest group were those with social, emotional, and behavioural difficulties.

A number of forces can be seen at play and these have their historical routes (see Box 1.2).

Box 1.2 Forces away from inclusion and towards inclusion
Issue or theme

Forces acting away from inclusion	Issue or theme	Forces acting towards inclusion
	Compulsory education for all children (1870, 1891) and extension of compulsory education	→
	Creation of special schools for particular groups of pupils (deaf, blind, maladjusted) bringing these children into education	→
←	Medicalization of special educational needs	
←	Defining some children as 'ineducable' and shifting responsibility out of education	
←	Development of a three-tier secondary system with additional special schoolsIntroduction of a comprehensive education system	→
←	Achievement agenda (payment by results, league tables) putting pressure on head teachers and schools	
	Introduction of school performance measures to take account of different starting levels and context (CVA)	→
	Plowden Report and Warnock Report focus on child-centred learning and the need to remove labels	→
	Warnock Report has emphasis on mainstream education	→
	Introduction of National Curriculum for all children including special schools	→
←	Expectations of pupil performance at Key Stages	
←	Quasi-market forces introduced to education	
←	Rigid inspection system for schools and teachers introduced	
	Teaching assistants provided as a support mechanism in mainstream schools	→
	Training and structure for teaching assistants	→
←	Deskilling of teachers through the increase in teacher assistant support	
	Staged approach to assessment through intervention and learning (redefining SEN as an educational issue)	→
←	Central government monitoring that relies on categorization of SEN retains elements of the medical model	
←	Funding arrangements via Statements	
	Delegated SEN budgets	→
	Training packages for teachers (e.g. Inclusion Development Programme)	→
	Centralized curriculum and support packages through a Waves model	→
	Initiatives, reports, and pilot studies commissioned by central government	→
←	Green Paper 2011 'removing the bias towards inclusion'	

Now, in 2011, we have a range of educational provision. We have segregated provision in some areas for particular types of pupil; we have units that pupils spend some time in and the remainder of the time in mainstream schools; we have units attached to mainstream schools; we have children in mainstream classes supported by teaching assistants; we have children in mainstream classes for most of the time with additional support as individuals or in small groups; we have some classes where the teacher thinks about inclusion of all pupils with diverse needs at the point of planning the lesson. Despite this, some children are not in the education system at all; their parents may educate them at home or they may have been excluded from school. We have an education system that marks some children out as being different and labels them as having problems defined as SEN. Vast amounts of money, time, and effort are spent on trying to reduce their problems and in education there is rhetoric of needing to 'narrow the gap'. The reason that we end up with such wide variation is the interplay between the different agendas acting at national, local, and personal levels. Not everyone shares the aspirational dream enshrined in the Dakar Agreement, and there is a definite shift away in government thinking (DfE, 2011b).

An alternative view is that children are different, and they do not have problems. Rather, the 'problems' exist in the context of the social relationship between the teacher, the learning environment, and the learner. This idea is not new: it is at the heart of Vygotsky's work and emphasizes the need to adapt teaching to the needs of the child so that the child can just succeed at a learning task with adult mediation (the zone of proximal development) (Vygotsky, 1978).

Imagine a different world – one that values all human beings whatever their abilities and treats all children with respect as learners. In this world we do not necessarily need to conceptualize special educational needs but could simply recognize individual differences and patterns of strengths as well as weaknesses. Individuals are valued for the varied contributions that they can make and teaching is geared to developing all individuals no matter what their starting point. This is a world that is socially inclusive and one in which teachers notice and adjust their teaching to match the needs of the children that they have in their class (rather than the children they want to have in their class). It is a world in which teachers are allowed to develop skills and expertise in supporting all pupils. In this world, professionals work together to help the teacher become more effective, whereas, in the real one, there is a temptation to see professionals that are 'experts' who 'treat' 'conditions'. What would that world look like and what would be the challenges that face teachers and schools? How would classrooms be different? Can we truly move towards a fully inclusive educational system with all children in mainstream schools?

In this book, we have asked leading academics and authors to think about an area in which they are experts and to draw out the challenges and competing agendas, to be controversial in their writing so that you, the reader, will be able to reflect on what is important and what might be possible in the context in which you work. Rather than doing this in a piecemeal way of thinking about children with problems, we are encouraging you to think holistically. Towards the end of the book we will ask you to reflect on what you have read and to design your future classroom in a step towards creating this world.

2

BARBARA RIDDICK
Labelling learners with 'SEND': the good, the bad and the ugly

The previous chapter has alluded to labelling as being a contentious issue in the field of education and particularly so when it comes to special educational needs. The intention of this chapter is to examine and question a number of assumptions that have arisen around the area of labelling and to deconstruct what labelling means to different individuals. An analysis as to the advantages and disadvantages of labelling children is also offered so that the reader can reflect on this issue in the context of the setting in which they work and their professional experience with children or young people.

A first point is that labelling is often portrayed in black and white terms and some educationalists propose that all labelling is inherently bad with the implication that not labelling is good. But it could be argued that labelling is a much more subtle and complex process that is an inherent part of everyday communication. Wilson (2007) points out that our language system is based on categorization and that whether we like it or not labelling is an integral part of how we can efficiently and effectively communicate with others. In the same way that many have argued that inclusion should be thought of as an ongoing process, I would argue that it is more helpful to think of labelling as a process and to consider what constitutes a helpful or unhelpful labelling process. Wilson suggests we can label wisely or unwisely, but that we cannot escape some sort of categorization. As with inclusion, it appears that the focus has been on whether to label or not rather than examining the quality of any labelling that takes place. This is not to suggest that we should be rushing around labelling children, but to think about the advantages and disadvantages of labelling an individual child at a given time in a given context.

Informal versus formal labelling

Teachers, like all individuals, exercise a great deal of informal categorization or labelling. A teacher may, for example, note those learners that need additional help, those learners who are inattentive, those learners who are particularly keen, and so on. Each teacher may have a different set of informal categories and may apply them in a different way. At one end of the continuum these informal categories or 'labels' may be private to the teacher and not shared with others. But even at this level, they may well influence how a teacher responds to a given child and influence their future perceptions of the child. At the next level, the teacher may more explicitly convey their categorization to the child or children in question or may share these labels with other teachers. A number of dyslexic children and older students are quite clear that some teachers called them 'lazy', 'stupid' or 'idiots' (Riddick, 2010). Many teachers, in contrast, use largely helpful or constructive categories that enable them to target their teaching more effectively. It can be argued that some categories such as 'needs motivating' can be essentially positive or negative depending on the spirit in which they are applied. If a teacher is using this as a reminder about a group of children that they as a teacher want to work harder to motivate, then this can be seen as a positive labelling process, whereas if this is largely being applied in a spirit of condemnation and dismissal, it could be seen as negative. This illustrates that even at this informal level of labelling, subtle and complex processes are at work. It can be argued that one of the advantages of informal labels is that they can be transient because they are not generally committed to paper or to formal discussion and they should be open to revision. Evidence on this point is mixed and although this may well be the case in some instances, there is also evidence that negative informal labelling can persist throughout a learner's time at school (Armstrong & Humphrey, 2009; Burden, 2008). A drawback of informal labels is that they are not open to the same level of scrutiny and questioning as more formal labels.

For formal labels, a considerable amount of evidence is required, often from a number of sources and this can be contested or questioned. It usually requires input from parents and the learner involved as well as a range of professionals (Frederickson & Cline, 2009). This is not of itself a reason for applying a formal label, but it does serve as a warning that informal labelling is not always benign and sometimes it can be based on inaccurate data, misunderstanding, and lack of appropriate information about a child. In practice, there is often a loose continuum from very informal to quite formal labelling, although within there is wide variation. For some children, a great deal of informal negative labelling can occur, often emanating from teachers, peers, and the wider community. Quicke and Winter (1994) suggest that constructs or informal labels like 'slow' or 'immature' are often taken for granted in the classroom and are frequently at an implicit rather than explicit level. Randall and Parker (1999) comment as to how important it is to have a full understanding of the labelling process and to be aware of assumptions applied on the basis of issues publically mentioned as well as those that are left unsaid. Hallahan and Kaufmann (1994, p. 54) comment that 'disabilities do not disappear simply by removing a label'.

Pros and cons

The general arguments for and against labelling have been well rehearsed within literature around this topic, but will be outlined here as a starting point for more in-depth discussion. When reading what follows, and in considering educational practice with children, it is important to bear in mind that much depends on what is meant by labelling and how well the process is carried out when thinking about positives and negatives.

Advantages of labelling:

- Acknowledging and accurately understanding a child's learning differences is a starting point for addressing their needs appropriately.
- Labels help those concerned to access a wide range of research on appropriate forms of intervention and support.
- Labels allow those with similar types of difference to develop their own culture and advocacy groups if they so wish.
- In some cases, a label can lead to greater self-understanding and empowerment.
- In some instances, labels act as mediators in that they explain behaviour that may seem culturally odd or unacceptable to the wider public, which should lead to greater tolerance and understanding.

Disadvantages of labelling:

- Inaccurate or unnecessary labels can lead to inappropriate interventions.
- Some labels are more likely to be unacceptable or unhelpful for individuals.
- Some labels are more likely to be viewed negatively by the general public and lead to further stigmatization.
- Labelling can 'blame' the child when other factors such as poor teaching or an inappropriate curriculum are responsible for the child's difficulties.
- Labels can be used as a way of controlling problematic or challenging groups of individuals.

There are inevitable grey areas in judging the appropriateness of labelling a child. Most current educationalists working in the UK would agree on the need for an inter-actional model of special educational needs (SEN) that acknowledges the importance of both environmental and within-child factors. This can lead to debate about the nature of the interaction between these factors and the relative weighting that should be given to them in individual cases. Is a child's poor reading largely due to inadequate teaching or to within-child processing difficulties that have led to slow progress despite good-quality teaching? All labels bring up the difficult question of where to draw the line in this judgement. This is where the question of the advantages and disadvantages of having a particular label become important to weigh up. An understandable concern (Oftsed, 2010) is that too many children are labelled as having special educational needs and disability (SEND), when in fact better quality teaching that caters for a wide range of learning abilities should address their needs and circumvent the need for a label. Whole-school monitoring of trends and patterns in learning should identify where teaching needs strengthening or the curriculum revising so as to effectively meet needs. In the USA, in particular, there has been considerable interest in the idea of 'response to intervention', such as in the area of reading. The argument is that if children are given additional rigorous and well-specified reading instruction, this should differentiate between children who can respond and make progress and keep on track without the need for a specific label and children who appear to have severe and enduring specific processing difficulties that warrant in US parlance a label of 'learning disability' or 'reading disability'. This brings up the issue of what label, if any, is most appropriate or acceptable to an individual within the cultural context in which they live. A learner with a similar profile in the UK would probably receive a specific learning difficulty or dyslexia label. Although there is support in both the UK and the USA for a response to instruction approach, critics point out that it still waits for children to fail and that with better early screening and assessment it is possible to identify at risk children at an earlier stage and put appropriate support in place before they begin to fail in the formal education system. It may be that a combination of these approaches is the best way forward.

Do labels stigmatize: the mediation effect

A frequent assumption around this topic is that labelling automatically leads to stigmatization and in some cases the two words are treated as if they are synonymous. It is revealing, therefore, to go back to Goffman's (1963) pioneering work on stigmatization and note that the issue of labelling in not raised whatsoever in his book. Goffman's research was focused on the stigmatization people felt as a direct consequence of the reactions of others and in the absence of an explicit label of which the onlooker was aware. Goffman documented a range of negative experiences and perceptions that people with widely varying disabilities encountered. Drawing on a range of research and autobiographies (e.g. Brown, 1954; Sainsbury, 2009), it is clear that stigmatization can be felt either by individuals who have lived, often for some time, without a specific label or long before an individual has been given a specific label. In cases like this, negatively perceived differences (by onlookers) referring to an individual's appearance, their skills, their behaviour or communication, seem to be the root cause of stigmatization. In some cases, people assume that it is a label that leads to stigmatization rather than appreciating that stigmatization already exists in society and that a label is simply encapsulating existing negative attitudes. Influential negative attitudes towards mental health might exemplify this point and have been disclosed by research based in the UK and elsewhere (Corrigan, 2006).

It does, however, suggest that withholding a label from an individual in the hope that this will somehow avoid stigmatization is, in such cases, like burying your head in the sand, thus denying the reality of everyday experiences and interactions. An important distinction that Goffman (1963) made was between what he called 'evident' and 'not evident' disabilities. An evident disability would be one that is readily seen and, to some degree, understood by an onlooker. So if we see someone sitting in a wheelchair, we realize they have a physical disability and do not consider them 'lazy' for sitting in a chair all day. Whereas if we encounter someone who makes direct personal comments such as 'you're very fat', we are likely to think them rude because it is not evident to us that this person has autism and is not intending to be insulting. To some extent, people with evident and not evident disabilities have different issues to deal with in their everyday lives. Those with evident disabilities have to encounter the re-actions of others on a daily basis and also often have an ongoing battle to be seen as a 'person' first rather than as a 'wheelchair user' or a blind person. For them, labels that precede them may add to this difficulty and therefore be something they do not want to use more than is necessary in public. In contrast, those with hidden or not evident disabilities are much more likely to encounter people making incorrect and negative attributions about their behaviour. In their case, labels may perform an important mediating function that allows people to understand and have a more positive view of their behaviour. People with not evident disabilities such as Tourette's syndrome, autism or dyslexia are often quite positive about their label because it allows them self-understanding and also, often, a greater degree of understanding and tolerance from others (MacDonald, 2010). The key question that should be asked is whether a label will decrease or increase the stigmatization an individual is experiencing. We have to accept that the answer to this question will not always be straightforward and individuals can have ambivalent and fluctuating views on the value of a particular label:

> I constantly weigh up its good and bad points. Most of the time it has been of benefit, about 80% of the time, 5% of the time I do think I'm not happy about being called dyslexic.
> (University student, cited in Riddick, Farmer, & Sterling, 1997, p. 32)

Living with labels

Living with a label and its day-to-day ramifications is an ongoing process and to label wisely we need to monitor and review this process and listen carefully to the views and reactions of those who are living with the label. Labelling wisely should be a collaborative process and it should start by asking the following questions:

- Is there a need for a label or, with better teaching, will the child's needs be met?
- Is the proposed label the most accurate and valid one available for their particular profile?
- Will the label in question lead to a better understanding of the child's needs?
- Will the label in question enable more effective forms of intervention to take place?
- Will the label in question allow the child to understand his or her own learning/behaviour better?
- Will the label allow the learner to feel more positive about themselves?
- Will the label give the learner access to peers with similar differences/difficulties if they so wish?
- Will the label allow them access to wider cultural support groups or networks if they so wish?
- Will the label help their parents to more effectively understand and support them?
- Will the label help the wider community to have a more positive and under-standing view of their differences/difficulties?

One of the problems with the above list is that some labels may be inherently more 'enabling' or better news than others. It is unlikely that a child who is told they have social, emotional, behavioural difficulties is going to feel particularly enabled, so there are real questions about the way different labels are perceived by children, their parents, their teachers, and the wider community (Mowat, 2009). But this again is a complex issue and a wide range of factors can influence how a student feels about a particular label. When we asked university students who had dyslexia about how they felt about the label, we found that the following factors played a part in how they felt:

- Those who already suspected they had a specific literacy difficulty were much more likely to be positive about the label.

- Those who initiated the assessment process or were pleased when someone else suggested they went for assessment were much more likely to be positive than those who were surprised by the suggestion.

- Those who thought they received adequate follow-up counselling were more likely to be positive.

- Those who rated their written report more positively were also more likely to rate the impact of the label 'dyslexia' more positively.

It could be that these factors often overlap or go hand in hand, but we did find instances where a student was initially negative about being assessed, but with a well-conducted assessment process and counselling they revised their opinion. Whereas the majority of the students were positive about the label 'dyslexia' and rated their self-esteem as enhanced, a minority (3 per cent) said it initially lowered their self-esteem, but several noted that over time as they understood more about dyslexia and it helped them study more effectively and understand themselves, they became increasingly positive about the label and thought their self-esteem was ultimately higher than before they were identified. One student, for example, said that initially she knew nothing about dyslexia and thought it was some sort of 'disease'. But after receiving counselling and support, she became very positive about the term and thought it had enabled her to study more effectively and feel much better about herself. She had volunteered to become a student ambassador and went into schools to speak positively about dyslexia and share her experiences as a way of offering support to children in school who were having similar difficulties to her own. Based on research with further education students, Armstrong and Humphrey (2009) suggested that different reaction patterns to such a label could be identified. Studies like this underline the need for more research into the impact of specific labels and the process by which someone acquires a label and the long-term consequences of that label for their academic performance and well-being. In research on dyslexic children, Humphrey (2002) found that those in special units with knowledgeable teachers who understood their difficulties had higher self-esteem than dyslexic children in mainstream classes who still felt their academic performance was viewed negatively by some of their teachers and peers. The dyslexic children in mainstream school generally had markedly lower self-esteem than their non-dyslexic classmates. Burden and Burdett (2005) reported similar results using the Myself as a Learner Scale (MALS).

They found that dyslexic children in mainstream school received an average score of 60.8, whereas non-dyslexic children received a score of 71. But when some of the dyslexic children transferred to a specialist dyslexia school in year 8 with an average score of 57.9, their scores gradually increased so that by grade 10 the average score was 68.5. Riddick (2010) found that although the majority of children she interviewed were positive about the label 'dyslexia', half of them didn't use the label openly at school because they felt teachers and peers were either hostile or lacked understanding of what the label meant. This suggests that it is also important to distinguish between the private and public aspects of a label and that at a private level a label may give self-understanding and access to sympathetic support groups even if it is of little help, or is a drawback in certain public settings such as some mainstream schools. One teenage girl with severe dyslexia made the following comment: 'People jump to the wrong conclusion and they should be educated about what dyslexia means. It's just been one of my dreams to tell them all what it means' (Riddick, 2010, p. 157). This is an argument used by various groups who have been discriminated against in the past: the need to own or reclaim particular labels and fight for a positive view of them, such as 'black' or 'gay'. It is significant that such labels are increasingly linked to positive identity and empowerment in the UK and elsewhere in the world.

Labels that enhance systems and people

Within the education system it can be argued that the move towards 'autism-friendly' or 'dyslexia-friendly' schools is part of this sensitization process. This encourages schools to change their practices and attitudes at a systemic level to make the school a much more enabling place for some previously marginalized groups of children to learn in. Part of this process emphasizes that labels should be accepted and used openly if children so wish. Paradoxically, in theory, the more 'autism friendly' or 'dyslexia friendly' a school becomes, the less need there may be for some children with milder difficulties to have a specific label, as their needs are more effectively met in a more accommodating educational setting. This, again, emphasizes the dynamic and ongoing nature of labelling as a process at this historical point. It may be that individuals wish to use a 'strong' form of a label when they think they are misunderstood and discriminated against and that as such social attitudes lessen, and understanding increases, there is less need for this. In this sense, some labels may have a strong educative function, drawing attention to the needs of specific groups of children and indicating how to meet their needs. Whether this has to be a perpetual process or with time can be embedded within ongoing teaching practice is currently unclear. In response, some educationalists have suggested that initial teacher training, in particular, should contain far more substantive content around SEN: one which prepares future teachers more thoroughly in meeting diverse learning needs (Nash & Norwich, 2010). As part of a move towards a more inclusive teaching culture some level of embedding should take place, but teachers have such a diverse range of needs to cater for that it is hard to see how they can deliver on so many disparate fronts without the specialist knowledge that certain labels allow them to access. Tobias (2009) reported on a successful support centre for students with autism spectrum disorders (ASDs) in a mainstream secondary school. She noted that 'a sound knowledge of ASD and the key characteristics of the condition that can impact on a student's education underlie the staff's ability to problem solve and plan well educationally' (Tobias, 2009, p. 160). Cann (2007) reported that secondary age children with autism/ASDs said that the label gave them a greater understanding of themselves and helped them to cope better in mainstream school. Individuals who are aware that they are different, and are aware that they are viewed negatively by others, and puzzled by aspects of their own behaviour can find it an immense relief to have a label that explains and makes sense of their problems and difficulties:

> Being diagnosed was a huge relief. Finally to have a name for it, to be able to say this is how Claire is and it's not that she's not trying hard enough or being deliberately difficult.
>
> (Sainsbury, 2009, p. 2)

This comment was made by Claire Sainsbury, who had a difficult time at school and, only as an adult, received a diagnosis of Asperger's syndrome. She went on to publish an influential book entitled *A Martian in the Playground* (2009), in which she documented her experiences and those of others with Asperger's in the school setting. This book won the NASEN (National Association of Special Educational Needs Teachers) book of the year award because as well as recounting their experiences, it made constructive suggestions for how teachers could better understand and support children with Asperger's syndrome. This underlines that for some individuals labels can be very helpful, and that practitioners can learn a great deal by listening to the experiences of such individuals.

The child is more than a label

An issue of concern when considering labels is who is doing the labelling and for what purpose (Riddick, 2000). Most educationalists would argue that their reasons for labelling or not labelling are driven by a benevolent desire to help children. However, sociologists such as Barton and Tomlinson (1984) argue that covert reasons such as power and control over resources may also be involved. In the past, children and their families had little power or control over this process but with changes in the SEN Code of Practice they, in theory at least, should have more of a say. Perhaps not surprisingly educationalists have framed their labels or categorizations within a learning context using terms such as 'learning disability' and 'reading disability', prevalent in the USA, and 'learning difficulty' and 'specific learning difficulty', widespread in the UK. Some have argued for largely curriculum process-based labels such as 'reading difficulty', 'writing difficulty', and 'spelling difficulty'. The problem with these is that a child with dyslexia, autism or hearing impairment could end up with a string of these process-based labels each with difficulty or disability at the end. This parcels the child out into separate processes and fails to understand the overarching reasons for their difficulties/differences.

It can be argued that labels like 'autism' and 'dyslexia' can combine process- and developmentally based perspectives, offering a more parsimonious explanation that addresses the needs of the whole child. It is only by having a deeper understanding of the underlying cognitive processes that lead to, for example, poor theory of mind or impaired phonological skills that more effective and targeted interventions can be developed. We know, for example, that children who have considerable difficulty learning to read despite adequate instruction are also likely to have persistent spelling problems and slower writing speed, which may well continue into adulthood. A label that unites these related difficulties and indicates a likely developmental pathway can further self-understanding and also map out likely educational needs and accommodations as a child progresses through school. A substantial concern relating to labels is that they encourage a stereotype and, consequently, the unique needs of children with the same label are overlooked or individual differences underemphasized. This goes back to the issue of viewing labelling as a process and questioning the quality of this process. Good practitioners tend to see labels as a jumping off point and constantly explore and question how a given child both differs and fits with the attributes ascribed to a particular label. Good labelling uses labels as signposts or pointers to relevant information and guidance but incorporates within it the need to constantly review and revise the appropriateness of a label for a particular child.

We are also probably moving towards a more relativistic view of certain labels. Even when we consider a relatively straightforward term like 'hearing impairment', it is apparent that this is on a continuum and that there are also qualitatively different forms of hearing loss such as high- and low-frequency hearing loss. It also indicates that hearing ability, reading ability, social skills, motor skills, spelling skills, and so on can all be on a continuum and differ qualitatively as well. This has led, for example, to the idea of an autistic spectrum with the term 'autistic spectrum disorder' being increasingly used in preference to the simple term 'autism'. There are inevitably dilemmas and contradictions in whatever label is used. Some would argue that the terms 'autism' or 'Asperger's syndrome' are better because they don't include disorder, deficit or impairment in the title and it is thus easier to appreciate the positive qualities or differences such individuals have and not focus exclusively on the idea of a deficit or impairment. Others would argue that it is important to have labels that underline the idea of a continuum or spectrum and the relativistic nature of certain labels. Although disabled people themselves can have widely differing views about labelling in general and their preferred label in particular (if any), a fundamental argument is that as they are the people who have to live with a label, they should be closely consulted about this and given as much control and power over this process as possible.

Translating this into the educational context suggests that we need to sensitively monitor the impact of particular labels on the children in question, as well as their peers, teachers, and parents. This sounds a simple undertaking but actually a range of variables have to be taken into account, including: the context of the labelling; pre-existing beliefs about the term for all those concerned; the age of the child; how the label has been negotiated and over what period of time; what actions and attitudes the label has led to both in school and in the wider community; how it has impacted on a child's educational performance, their social interactions, and self-efficacy as a learner; and whether it has enhanced their personal understanding and well-being. For some children, the impact of a label may vary over time and educational circumstances, and much will depend on how well it has been operationalized over the long term. This suggests that longitudinal research looking at how they feel about a label and its attendant consequences over a period of time and educational phases will be especially valuable. Some children want labels used in a subtle and understated way that appreciates their difficulties and meets their needs without embarrassing them or underlining their differences to other children. Many teachers are aware of these contradictions and realize the need to exercise caution and tact when applying labels. The way in which teachers use labels to attend to children's needs on a day-to-day basis has not been extensively researched but what research exists indicates large individual differences between teachers (Ireson & Hallum, 2001). If we wish to understand more about what constitutes a good labelling process (including knowing when not to label), more research on this issue is required. In a similar vein, we know that, especially with younger children, parents often play an important if not leading role in this process. Again there has been relatively little research on this issue. Riddick (2010) found in the case of dyslexia and school aged children that the majority named their parents and especially their mothers as the people who had initially explained dyslexia to them. With children in particular, we have to separate out what a specific label indicates to significant adults in their life and how children themselves perceive the label over time.

In summary, it can be suggested that a more considered and nuanced approach to labelling and the labelling process is needed that recognizes that it can have positive, negative, and sometimes ambiguous outcomes.

3

PETER FARRELL

Inclusive education for children with special educational needs: current uncertainties and future directions

Introduction

A key aspect of the Labour government's education policy (1997–2010) was actively to promote inclusive education for children with special educational needs (SEN). This formal commitment was proclaimed in 1997 through the publication of the Special Educational Needs Green Paper, *Excellence for All Children* (DfEE, 1997). From then on, this commitment was restated, strengthened, and given operational forms many times, in particular by the guidance on *Inclusive Schooling: Children with Special Educational Needs* (DfES, 2001a, 2001b), the SEN strategy document *Removing Barriers to Achievement* (DfES, 2004b), and through the roll out of initiatives designed to improve the quality of inclusive education in schools, such as the Inclusion Development Programme (DfE, 2010c) and *Achievement for All* (DfE, 2010a). The Labour government's policy on inclusion reflected international developments in this area that were given substantial impetus 16 years ago when the Salamanca World Conference on Special Needs Education endorsed the idea of inclusive education (UNESCO, 1994a, 1994b). The subsequent Salamanca Statement was arguably the most significant international document that has ever appeared in the field of special education. It stated that regular schools with an inclusive orientation are 'the most effective means of combating discriminatory attitudes, building an inclusive society and achieving education for all'. Furthermore, it suggested that such schools can 'provide an effective education for the majority of children and improve the efficiency and ultimately the cost-effectiveness of the entire education system' (UNESCO, 1994a, para. 3). Subsequent pressure from governments and international organizations around the world to develop inclusive special education systems have been mirrored by a large number of publications that have extolled the values of inclusion and which have provided a whole range of accounts of 'good practice' in inclusive education (see, for example, Ainscow et al., 2006; Ainscow & Miles, 2008; Ballard, 1999; Chapman, Ainscow, Miles, & West, in press; Forlin & Lian, 2008; Giangreco, 2006; Mittler, 2000).

Farrell and colleagues (Farrell, Dyson, Polat, Hutcheson, & Gallannaugh, 2007) and MacBeath and co-workers (MacBeath, Galton, Steward, MacBeath, & Page,

2006) suggested that the principles underlying the development of inclusive education received a good deal of consensual support from teachers, parents, and local
education authority officers in the UK. However, these authors argue that there was
much less agreement about whether these principles could be realized in practice and,
even if they could, there was concern about what the impact of inclusive education
might be on the achievements of pupils without SEN in mainstream schools and on
their peers. Concerns about the effectiveness of inclusive education have also been
reflected by Ofsted reports on special education (Ofsted, 2006, 2010), both of which
consistently refer to the variable quality of inclusive practices in mainstream schools.
Perhaps it is not surprising, therefore, that the new Coalition government has raised
some questions about the apparent trend towards inclusion. This was stimulated by a
report commissioned by the Conservative Party (Balchin, 2007) and reinforced in the
Green Paper on special educational needs and disability (SEND) (DfE, 2011b). This
consultation paper makes three references to the Coalition government's intention to
'remove the bias towards inclusion' with the implication that, in the recent past,
parents have been strongly encouraged to accept a placement for their child in an
'inclusive' setting as opposed to a special school. The Green Paper stresses the
Coalition government's commitment to provide parents with more choice over where
their child should be educated. At the time of writing, the Green Paper is 'out for
consultation', a process that was due to be completed in September 2011. But it is
possible that some of the recommendations and suggestions made in the Green Paper,
including those that refer to inclusive education, will shape the future direction of
provision for pupils with SEN over the next ten years.

Whatever the outcomes of the consultation on the Green Paper, with regard to
inclusive education, its publication signals a significant shift in the tone of the discussions. Between 1997 and 2010, all government documents on education referred to
inclusive education in positive terms as a principle that should be implemented in
practice. But now, in the UK, we are receiving a different message, one that states that
the bias towards inclusion will be removed! Those silent voices, which in the past
might have expressed strong opinions about the value of segregated education systems
for pupils with SEN, can now speak more freely in the knowledge that these views
will receive a sympathetic hearing from government ministers. But there are also well-
known advocates of inclusive education whose views will continue to be heard. Hence,
one consequence of the Green Paper is that the debate about inclusive education will
be reignited.

The first part of this chapter considers the evolution of the concept of inclusive
education for pupils with SEN and shows how this evolution has resulted in two
complementary but distinct definitions. One of these defines inclusion in terms of the
numbers of pupils attending mainstream schools who would previously have attended
special schools. The second focuses on the quality of education received by pupils
with SEN in mainstream schools, the majority of whom have always attended such
schools. The chapter goes on to discuss the trends in the numbers of pupils attending
special schools and briefly reviews research evidence on the impact of placing such
pupils in mainstream environments. This is followed by a review of the origin and of
some of the consequences of defining inclusion in terms of improving the quality of
education for pupils with SEN in mainstream schools. The chapter concludes with

some reflections on the possible consequences of the Green Paper for the future direction of inclusive education in this country.

The evolving concept of inclusive education

Definitions of inclusion within the educational context have varied, representing diverse perspectives and ideologies (e.g. Clair, Church, & Bateshaw, 2002; Falvey, Givner, & Kimm, 2005; Gee, 2004; Giangreco, 2006; Lewis & Doorlag, 2006; Turnbull, Turnbull, Erwin, & Soodak, 2006). Indeed, up until the early 1990s, the word 'inclusion' was hardly used. Instead, the terms 'integration' or 'mainstreaming' were employed and these referred exclusively to the placement of pupils attending special schools in regular education classes in mainstream schools. There were, of course, different degrees of integration, from full-time placement of a child with disabilities in a mainstream class in his or her local school (functional integration) to the placement of a pupil in a special class or unit attached to a mainstream school (locational integration) (Hegarty, 1991).

The rationale for integration, defined in this way, is reflected in literature going back many years, much of which stresses the rights of all children no matter how disabled to attend a mainstream school. For example, the Centre for Studies on Inclusive Education (1989) advocated the following view forcibly in their Integration Charter:

> We see the ending of segregation in education as a human rights issue which belongs within equal opportunities policies. Segregation in education because of disability or learning difficulty is a contravention of human rights as is segregation because of race and gender. The difference is that while sexism and racism are widely recognized as discrimination . . . discrimination on the grounds of disability or learning difficulty is not.

Other writers took a similar view (see, for example, Hall, 1996; Jupp, 1992) and many used strong language to describe special schools, describing them as perpetuating a form of educational apartheid that devalues the children placed in them and denies them opportunities afforded to pupils in mainstream schools.

A key illustration of the influence of these arguments on shaping policy is clause 4 of the Salamanca Statement (UNESCO, 1994a), which stresses that children with 'special educational needs must have access to regular schools'. This position is strongly reinforced by the Special Needs and Disability Act 2001, which states that a child with SEN and a Statement *must* (my emphasis) be educated in a mainstream school unless this would be incompatible with (a) the wishes of the parents or (b) the provision of efficient education of other children (HMSO, 2001).

Although definitions of inclusion that focus on the placement of children with SEN in a mainstream context have been adopted in government policy documents, a problem with definitions of this sort is that they do not say anything about the quality of the education that is offered to pupils. Are pupils placed in units attached to a mainstream school (an example of locational integration) more 'included' than if they were taught in a special school? Jupp (1992) argued that such units can be just as segregating.

Indeed, even pupils placed in a regular mainstream class may be isolated from the rest of the class and not truly 'integrated' within the group, particularly if they work with a support worker or teaching assistant in one-to-one sessions for the majority of each day. Inclusive placements, therefore, may still leave the pupil 'segregated' (Harrower, 1999).

Partly for these reasons, the term 'inclusion' became used as a way of describing the extent to which a pupil, categorized as needing to receive special education services, is truly 'integrated'. Used in this way, the term refers to the extent to which a school or community welcomes such pupils as full members of the group and values them for the contribution that they make. This implies that for inclusion to be seen to be 'effective', all pupils with disabilities must actively belong to, be welcomed by, and participate in a mainstream school and community. Their diversity of interests, abilities, and attainment should be welcomed and be seen to enrich the school community.

Giangreco (2006) reflects this broader view of inclusion and offers a definition that addresses all students, describes special education as a process, highlights the rights of students, emphasizes the responsibilities of all schools and education professionals, and recognizes that the school is a community context.

In the UK, definitions of inclusion have widened still further. Booth and Ainscow (1998), for example, took the view that policies on inclusion should not be restricted to the education of pupils thought to have special needs. Inclusion, they argued, is a process in which schools, communities, local authorities, and governments strive to reduce barriers to the participation and learning for all citizens. Looked at in this way, inclusive policies and practices should consider ways in which marginalized groups in society, such as people from ethnic minorities and those who are socially and economically disadvantaged, can participate fully in the educational process within mainstream contexts.

This view of inclusion is also reflected in guidance from school inspectors (Ofsted, 2000). In addressing what it refers to as 'educational inclusion', Ofsted focuses attention on a wide range of vulnerable groups. The guidance states:

> An educationally inclusive school is one in which the teaching and learning, achievements, attitudes and well-being of every young person matters. Effective schools are educationally inclusive schools. This shows, not only in their performance, but also in their ethos and their willingness to offer new opportunities to pupils who may have experienced previous difficulties . . . The most effective schools do not take educational inclusion for granted. They constantly monitor and evaluate the progress each pupil makes. They identify any pupils who may be missing out, difficult to engage, or feeling in some way apart from what the school seeks to provide.
>
> (Ofsted, 2000, p. 65)

Ofsted's guidance is important for two reasons. First, it reinforces a much broader view of inclusion in that the concept is widened to include pupils other than those thought to have SEN. Second, it forces schools to focus on the achievements of all of their pupils and, indeed, to pay attention to a wider range of outcomes than those reflected in test or examination results. (To my knowledge, Ofsted has not changed or updated its guidance since 2000.)

One way of defining inclusion that is in line with the above Ofsted definition is to conceptualize the issue around the following pupil outcomes in relation to inclusion: presence, acceptance, participation, and achievement.

- *Presence* refers to extent to which pupils attend lessons in mainstream settings in local schools and committees (this is similar to the previous notion of 'integration').
- *Acceptance* refers to the extent to which other staff and pupils welcome all pupils as full and active members of their community.
- *Participation* refers to the extent to which all pupils contribute actively in all the school's activities.
- *Achievement* refers to the extent to which pupils learn and develop positive views of themselves.

It is argued that for a school to be truly inclusive, all four conditions should apply to all children regardless of their abilities and disabilities and of their ethnic origin, social class or gender. It is not, for example, sufficient for children to be simply *present* in a school. They need to be *accepted* by their peers and by staff, they need to *participate* in all the school's activities, and they need to attain satisfactory levels of *achievement* in their work and behaviour. This formulation is proactive in the sense that it sets goals for schools, local authorities, communities, and governments and can act as a benchmark against which to judge the extent to which inclusive policies and practices are working.

A number of local authorities have adopted this or similar definitions of inclusion in their policy documents. For example, Orkney Council (2011) states that:

> Inclusion is the continuous process of increasing the presence, participation and achievement of all learners in education establishments. This requires schools to routinely and regularly review and reflect on their approaches for meeting the needs of those who are at greater risk of marginalization, exclusion and under-achievement in order to improve learning and teaching in a way which is a benefit to all. Through this process, which invokes a commitment to continuous improvement, the school accepts and learns from diversity and the uniqueness of the individual.

It is hard to argue against the principles and aspirations expressed in the broad and all-encompassing definitions of inclusive education reflected in the above discussion. No parent, teacher, local authority officer or government minister is likely to argue against the notion that all children from whatever background should be present, accepted, participate, and achieve in schools. Neither would they quarrel with the notion that schools have a responsibility to offer the highest quality education to all learners from a variety of backgrounds and with a range of diverse needs.

However, as highlighted in the 2006 House of Commons Select Committee's Third Report on SEN (House of Commons Education and Skills Committee, 2006), this broad definition is not particularly helpful in relation to the education of pupils with SEN. The report argues that:

> when it [inclusion]is defined as being about creating schools with an inclusive approach or ethos so that all children in the school are actively involved, playing a full and positive role in the classroom and with their peers, few would argue against such a principle or aim.
>
> (para. 62)

However, the report also makes the point that other government documents indicate a continued role for special schools and that they would only anticipate a gradual reduction in the number of such schools. Hence it takes issue with the confused messages and comments on the extent to which the government's aims for inclusive education for pupils with SEN appears to be evolving and changing, in particular Lord Adonis's statement that it was up to local authorities to decide on their policies on the continued existence of special schools, a direct contradiction from earlier guidance in the government's 2004 SEN strategy document, which advocated for a reduction in the number of special schools. In an attempt to bring some clarity to the debate, the 2006 Select Committee Report went on to state that it:

> supports the principle of educators pursuing an ethos that fully includes all children – including those with SEN and disabilities – in the setting or settings that best meets their needs and helps them achieve their potential, preferably a good school within their local community.
>
> (para. 64)

Hence, in the committee's view, a child with SEN can be 'included' if he or she is placed in a special school – if that is the setting that *best meets their needs*. This position is totally opposite to the conventional view that, in a fully inclusive education system, all pupils with SEN would be placed in a mainstream school. All the committee seems to be saying is that children with SEN should receive a high-quality education in a local school, but that this could be any type of school: special, mainstream, resourced unit, etc. Under this definition, there would be no need to consider closing special schools, provided that they offered high-quality education to their children.

Given the confusion in the Labour government's policy on inclusive education for children with SEN as reflected in the 2006 Select Committee Report, it is hardly surprising that the recent 2011 Green Paper takes an ambivalent, if slightly hostile view of inclusion. The phrase 'remove the bias towards inclusion' suggests that inclusive education might not be in the best interests of children with SEN, but that parents are under pressure to accept placements in mainstream schools. It is also interesting that the Green Paper makes no attempt to define inclusion – but the clear implication in the document is that inclusion should solely be defined in terms of providing education for *all* children with SEN in a mainstream school. Statements about removing the bias towards inclusion are simply about 'bias' to place children with SEN in mainstream schools. This is back to the original definition of integration. All the arguments about inclusion being a process whereby the whole school and community have a responsibility to provide the highest quality education for all learners, including children with SEN, do not receive a mention.

The above discussion indicates that there are two complementary but distinctive definitions of inclusive education in relation to pupils with SEN. The first defines inclusion as being to do with the closure of special schools and the relocation of children placed in them to a mainstream setting, similar to early definitions of integration. The second definition refers less to the place where pupils with SEN are taught and more to the quality of education they receive. It is not exclusively about improving the quality of education for pupils who have moved from special to mainstream schools, it also focuses as much on the education of children with SEN who have always been educated in mainstream schools. Hence inclusion, defined in this way, is a process of school improvement, where efforts are directed to support pupils with SEN in mainstream contexts. This approach to inclusive education is reflected in the Ofsted definition referred to above and in the Index for Inclusion (Booth & Ainscow, 2002). The 2006 Select Committee Report acknowledged this broader view of inclusion as being aspirational and not particularly controversial. There are also a number of publications that report on ways of promoting effective inclusive practice in schools (see, for example, Ainscow et al., 2006; Howes, Davies, & Fox, 2009).

In summary, therefore, inclusive education for children with SEN can be defined as (1) the placement of children with special needs in mainstream schools, or (2) a process that aims to improve the quality of education offered to pupils with SEN, some of whom might in the past have attended special schools but the majority will have always attended mainstream schools. In the next two sections of the chapter, I comment on the consequences, if any, that these two definitions of inclusive education have had for policy, practice, and research.

Inclusion as providing education for all children with SEN in mainstream schools

As stated above, the 2011 Green Paper (DfE, 2011b) makes no attempt to define inclusion. But the clear implication in the document is that inclusion should solely be defined in terms of placing children with SEN, who might otherwise attend a special school, in a mainstream school – that is, it adopts the first of the two definitions discussed above. The idea that there has been a *bias* towards inclusion, defined in this way, is evident in Labour government documents (1997–2010) and in the Special Needs and Disability Act, which instructed local authorities to place all children with SEN in mainstream schools, provided certain conditions were met. But is this so-called 'bias' reflected in the figures? Has there been a trend to educate increasing numbers of pupils with SEN in mainstream schools? On the whole, the government's own figures indicate that there has been no such trend and that the number of pupils in special schools has remained more or less static over the past 15 years. For example, paragraph 42 of the Green Paper states that 'the number of special schools has decreased from 1,161 in 2002 to 1,054 in 2010', which represents a modest decrease of 107 special schools over a period of eight years. As there are over 160 local authorities in England and Wales, this represents an average drop in the number of special schools of less than one per local authority since 2002. Furthermore, paragraph 42 of the

Green Paper goes on to state that 'the proportion of pupils with statements placed in them (special schools) has increased slightly in recent years, from 40 per cent in 2006 to 44 per cent in 2010. In 2006, 89,390 pupils were on roll in maintained and non-maintained special schools, this increased to 90,760 in 2010.' Looking further back, the House of Commons Education and Skills Select Committee Report on SEN (2006) provides figures for the number of pupils placed in special schools from 1991 to 2005. Chart 4 of that document indicates that there was a slight *increase* in the number of pupils in special schools during that period. Overall, therefore, there are *more* pupils in special schools in 2011 than there were in 1991, hardly a bias towards inclusion! An inescapable conclusion from the above analysis is that, despite the Labour government's 'initiatives' and the requirements of the Special Educational Needs and Disability Act 2001, the situation in relation to the placement of pupils with SEN in special schools remains more of less the same. Put simply, there has been no major change in the numbers of pupils placed in special schools over the last 20 years.

So what are we to make of these statistics? Clearly, there have been messages in the media and from some political parties (e.g. the Conservative Party manifesto leading up to the 2010 general election) suggesting that there have been mass closures of special schools, and that it was now time to reverse this trend. This is also reflected in the tone of the recent Green Paper, in which the government appears to ignore its own figures by stating that there has been a 'bias' towards inclusion. The fact that the statistics over the last 20 years indicate that the numbers of pupils in special schools has remained the same has, for some reason, been ignored. It looks as though, as a nation, we have started to believe the overpowering rhetoric, reflected in government documents and other literature promoting inclusion. It is also possible that we have interpreted the rise in the number of pupils identified with SEN in mainstream schools as evidence that there has been a corresponding drop in the numbers of such pupils attending special schools.

The statistics on the stable numbers of pupils in special schools raise another question. Why, despite strong government support for placing pupils with SEN in mainstream schools and concerted action from groups such as the Centre for Studies on Inclusive Education, has so little happened? There are two possible reasons. First, there is anecdotal evidence from some local authorities indicating that parents of children attending special schools have expressed great resistance to the prospect that their special school might close and they energetically, and very publically, lobby their local authority. Hence local authorities that have attempted to close special schools have encountered many obstacles. Second, there is a lack of research evidence suggesting that placing children who would otherwise have attended a special school in a mainstream context brings benefits to the children (for reviews of research, see Farrell, 2000; Harrower, 1999; Lindsay, 2007). Even though it is notoriously difficult to conduct rigorous scientific studies in this field, in relation to outcomes for pupils with SEN there is mixed evidence supporting the placement of such children in mainstream schools. Some studies suggest that there may be social benefits associated with inclusive placements but few, if any, in relation to academic attainments. Furthermore, the evidence on parents' views about inclusive education is extremely mixed with, as mentioned above, almost universal hostility to mainstream placements from parents of children who already attend a special school. There is also evidence that teachers in mainstream schools, although positive about the principles of inclusive education, are sceptical about how this can work in practice, particularly for children with severe emotional and behavioural problems. Hence ambivalent research evidence and pressure from parents to maintain special schools could explain why there has been almost no change in the numbers of pupils attending special schools over the last 20 years.

Inclusion as a process that aims to improve the quality of education offered to pupils with SEN in mainstream schools

Defining inclusion as a process that is concerned with improving the quality of education for pupils with SEN in mainstream schools has its origins in the Warnock Report (DES, 1978), which introduced the idea that up to 20 per cent of pupils might at any one time have SEN, 18 per cent of whom had always attended a mainstream school. Although not without controversy, this conceptualization of SEN has had a major impact on approaches to assessment and provision offered by mainstream schools to support the '18 per cent' of pupils who have SEN. For example, the 1981 Education Act introduced the staged process of identification and assessment of these pupils that has, following subsequent SEN legislation and codes of practice, become known as 'School Action', 'School Action Plus', and 'Statement'. Schools are obliged to maintain a register of pupils on each of these stages. Furthermore, schools employ special educational needs coordinators (SENCos) who coordinate support for pupils with SEN in mainstream schools. Hence a function for all mainstream schools is to ensure that they provide high-quality assessment and provision for children with SEN who have always been educated in these schools. This function has become synonymous with the provision of high-quality 'inclusive education' for these pupils.

Key aspects of the special educational legislation, in particular the statutory assessment procedures, have reinforced this role. Figures in the Select Committee Report (House of Commons Education and Skills Committee, 2006) indicate that, between 1991 and 2000, there was an increase of 95,000 in the number of Statements issued to pupils in mainstream schools, representing over 90 per cent of the total increase in the number of statemented pupils over this period. Since 1997, the numbers of Statements issued to pupils in mainstream schools has fallen slightly, although it remains at 54 per cent of the total number of Statements (DfE, 2011b). Historically, one of the reasons for this increase has to do with the financial help that is provided to schools that support these children. Typically local authorities, and not schools, have paid for the additional support that is provided for pupils with Statements in mainstream schools and this may have acted as an incentive to such schools to request statutory assessments in the knowledge that more help would be provided to them for which they did not have to pay. Hence schools' growing requests for statutory assessments resulted in increases in the number of Statements being issued for pupils in mainstream schools. In recent years, there has also been an increase in the number of pupils being placed on 'School Action' or 'School Action Plus', from 10 per cent to 18 per cent of all pupils since 1995. Increases in the numbers of pupils in mainstream schools being identified with SEN may have led the current Coalition government to believe that there has been a bias towards inclusion – omitting to point out that these pupils have always been educated in mainstream schools. The only difference is that procedures such as the Code of Practice, and definitions of inclusion that focus on improving the quality of education to all children in mainstream schools, have, quite rightly, focused attention on how schools support pupils who are experiencing difficulties.

The need to ensure that pupils with SEN received high-quality education in mainstream schools (i.e. were fully included) has also led to a number of other key developments. One of these is the huge rise in the numbers of teaching assistants who are currently employed by mainstream schools, many of whom support pupils with SEN. As referred to in Chapter 1 of this book, the number of teaching assistants has increased from 97,000 in 1998 to 180,000 in 2010. Indeed, it is not uncommon for there to be as many teaching assistants working in primary schools as there are teachers. On the whole, parents and teachers welcome the introduction of teaching assistants (Balchin, 2007; Blatchford et al., 2009a, 2009b). Despite the fact their conditions of service and salary are much less favourable than those of teachers, evidence from teaching assistants themselves and from teachers and head teachers suggests that their work is highly valued and that they make an extremely positive overall contribution to the running of a school. Despite this positive view of teaching assistants' work, there is contradictory evidence about their impact on raising the attainments of pupils, including pupils with SEN. Blatchford et al. (2009a, 2009b), for example, have found that, when all other variables are taken into account, there is a negative relationship between the numbers of teaching assistants employed in a school and the attainments of its pupils; that is, schools with more teaching assistants had lower attaining pupils than schools employing fewer teaching assistants. Farrell et al. (2010), however, reviewed a number of high-quality studies which indicated that, when teaching assistants received training and support to help pupils in a specific area, they were successful in significantly raising the pupils' academic attainments. Hence it may well be the case that simply placing teaching assistants in a mainstream school without providing them with adequate training and support may not make the anticipated positive difference to pupils' attainments.

As further encouragement to mainstream schools to improve the overall quality of inclusive education, the Labour government introduced a number of packages and materials that are designed to help teachers to improve the quality of their work with pupils with SEN in mainstream schools. One of these is the Inclusion Development Programme, a set of online resources and materials that target pupils with particular needs, such as specific language impairment, dyslexia, and autism (DfE, 2010c). A further initiative is *Achievement for All*, which comprises a set of materials for local authorities and mainstream schools that are aimed at raising attainments of pupils with SEN (DfE, 2010a). In addition to these materials and online resources, schools and local authorities have been provided with funds to employ staff to support their implementation in mainstream schools. For example, *Achievement for All* has been introduced into ten local authorities; each has received funding, much of which has been allocated directly to its schools (Humphrey & Squires, 2010, 2011). The programme was to be introduced in all local authorities in England and Wales in the autumn of 2011.

The increase in the number of teaching assistants, together with the introduction of packages and materials to support pupils with SEN in mainstream schools, reflects the consequences of defining inclusive education in terms of improving the quality of education for pupils with SEN, most of whom have always attended mainstream schools. And, indeed, as indicated in the Select Committee Report (House of Commons Education and Skills Committee, 2006), this aspirational definition is not, of itself, particularly controversial. However, when set alongside the agendas faced by all schools to raise the attainments of all their pupils, sometimes referred to as the 'Standards Agenda', it is easy to see how some schools might prioritize this agenda over their efforts to improve their inclusive practices. Indeed, there is substantial concern in the literature (see, for example, Dyson, Farrell, Polat, Hutcheson, & Gallanaugh, 2004; Lunt & Norwich, 1999) reflecting teachers' anxieties that, if they devote too much attention to providing high-quality inclusive education for pupils with SEN, this will have a negative impact on the overall attainments of the pupils and hence threaten the school's position in the 'league tables'. Fortunately, research evidence (see, in particular, Farrell et al., 2007) indicates that, when other variables are taken into account, there should be no negative impact on the academic performance of pupils in mainstream schools that is associated with increasing the number of pupils with SEN who are educated in such schools. Hence schools should feel confident in striving to provide high-quality inclusive education for its pupils with SEN without being concerned about the negative impact this might have on other pupils' attainments.

Conclusion – where do we go from here?

It is clear from the preceding discussion that there has been a great deal of uncertainty about the definition of inclusive education. This is reflected in the Select Committee Report and also, though not so explicitly, in the recent Green Paper on SEN. Defining inclusive education in terms of reducing the numbers of pupils in special schools has always been controversial. Despite government documents, international literature, and the work of active pressure groups, there is a great deal of concern from parents about threatened closure of special schools, and research literature in support of inclusive education, defined in this way, is, at best, inconclusive. Definitions of inclusive education that emphasize the process of improving the quality of education for pupils with SEN are much less controversial. All schools have a duty to provide high-quality education for all their children, including those who may experience difficulties in learning and behaviour. In recent years, government legislation and associated guidance, together with the introduction of a variety of support materials to schools has helped them to improve their work in this area. This is also an area in which research has the potential to inform and improve practice; for example, both the Inclusion Development Programme (DfE, 2010c) and *Achievement for All* (DfE, 2010a) are currently being evaluated and the findings will help in the development of future work in this area.

At this stage of the consultation process on the Green Paper, it is difficult to predict how services for children with SEN will develop and what influence the debates on inclusive education will have on this. The message in the Green Paper is that inclusion has gone far enough! But it defines inclusion, by implication, in terms of closing more special schools. It is vitally important to bring clarity to this aspect of the Green Paper's message and to reinforce the fact that there has been no change in the special school population in the past twenty years. Reducing the so-called 'bias' towards inclusion could result in a substantial rise in the number of pupils placed in special provision if mainstream schools, parents, and local authorities decide to respond to the Green Paper's message. In my view, this would be a backward step and run counter to developments in other countries.

The Green Paper considers that the 'bias' towards inclusion could be arrested if parents were given more choice in the school that their child should attend. The paper states that:

> Parents of children with statements of SEN will be able to express a prefer-ence for any state-funded school – including special schools, Academies and Free Schools – and have their preference met unless it would not meet the needs of the child, be incompatible with the efficient education of other children, or be an inefficient use of resources.
>
> (para. 7)

The intention seems to be that, by giving parents more choice, they will feel more involved in the assessment process, they will be made aware of the full range of options, including segregated provision, and that as a result, there will be less uncer-tainty and fewer conflicts with local authorities about selecting the appropriate provi-sion for their child. Hopefully, the outcomes will be in line with this well meant intention. However, what the Green Paper fails to discuss is the issue of who decides whether their preference 'would not meet the needs of the child, be incompatible with the efficient education of other children, or be an inefficient use of resources'. Inevitably, these decisions have to be made by the funder of the provision – currently the local authority, which takes advice from a number of professionals, including educational psychologists. There may be several reasons why the local authority may feel obliged to make a decision about provision for a pupil with SEN that is at odds with the wishes of the parents, particularly if those undertaking an assessment consider that the parents' preferred choice of provision would not meet the child's needs. Similarly, the local authority has a responsibility to keep within its budget, and the authority may consider that the cost of educating the child in accordance with the parents' wishes may be too high and take too much of their resources away from supporting other children with SEN for whom they are responsible. Of course, none of these problems is new. Local authorities have always tried to take parents' wishes into account, together with the needs of the pupils and the efficient use of resources. It is doubtful whether suggestions made in the Green Paper will have any effect on reducing the real concerns expressed by parents and, as a result, there will be some who continue to complain their views and wishes have not been taken into account.

But let us suppose that the intentions expressed in the Green Paper to reduce the bias towards inclusion become a reality. Presumably, this would mean that more parents, who have apparently felt bullied into accepting a mainstream placement for their child, would have their wishes for a special school placement acceded to by the local authority. However, as research indicates, many extremely articulate parents will continue to lobby for mainstream provision, and presumably, in line with the intentions expressed in the Green Paper, their wishes would also be met. The likely outcome will be that the cost of providing high-quality education for pupils with SEN, whether that is in a mainstream or special school, will rise as local authorities meet parents' conflicting wishes. Unless the Coalition government it prepared to increase its funding for SEN provision, local authorities will continue to struggle to meet their legal obligations under the SEN legislation to assess and provide for the education of pupils with SEN and, at the same time, keep within their budget.

In the meantime, as schools, parents, and local authorities struggle to come to terms with the implications of the message about inclusive education that is reflected in the Green Paper, mainstream schools should continue in their efforts to provide high-quality education for all their pupils, including those with SEN. Although the introduction of *Achievement for All* (DfE, 2010a) across England is a good sign, the Green Paper also suggests that the staged process of identification of pupils with SEN (School Action, School Action Plus, and Statements) should be overhauled. This may not necessarily be a negative step but, if a consequence of the Green Paper is that efforts to support pupils with SEN in mainstream schools are reduced, this will be unfortunate for large numbers of vulnerable children and their families across the country. Hence it is important to be vigilant and to do all we can to maintain our efforts to support pupils with SEN in mainstream schools in the future.

4

ALAN DYSON
Special educational needs and the 'world out there'

This chapter is predicated on the argument that much of the policy and many of the practices that are characteristic of special needs education embody a somewhat limited understanding of why children experience educational difficulties and what needs to be done to address those difficulties. Specifically, special needs education confuses educational issues that arise from the individual characteristics of learners with issues arising, in the case of many of its intended beneficiaries, from other sources entirely. These sources lie not in the constitution of the individual learner, but in the 'world out there', in the form of family dynamics, community cultures and, more broadly, in the complex phenomenon that is often labelled as 'social disadvantage'. The consequence of this confusion is that the interventions that are brought to bear to tackle learners' difficulties have only limited impacts, and schools and teachers are unable to help their students learn and prosper. Far from developing a fine-grained understanding of the 'whole child', therefore, special needs education has long *mis*understood most of the learners in its care.

In this chapter, I draw heavily on policy developments in England over recent years. This is partly because special needs provision here is overall of good quality – at least compared with many other countries – and, therefore, the fundamental limitations of special needs education are less likely to be hidden by more superficial problems to do with resourcing or organization. Largely, however, it is because, between 1997 and 2010, England had a centre-left 'New Labour' government that prioritized educational reform and paid particular attention to the relationship between social and educational disadvantage. While these reforms may well have been far from perfect (see, for instance, contributors to Chapman & Gunter, 2009, for a critical analysis), I wish to argue that they open up new possibilities for how the role of special needs education might in future be understood.

Schooling and educational inequalities in England

The English education system has many virtues and has, arguably, improved its performance significantly in recent years. However, it remains worryingly unequal in terms of the outcomes it produces for its students. If some young people achieve outstanding examination results, go on to 'top' universities, and enjoy rich life chances, others learn little at school, achieve no useful qualifications, leave at the first opportunity, and have correspondingly limited chances in their adult lives.

To some extent, these inequalities are attributable to individual characteristics and circumstances. However, it is also the case that they are socially patterned in important ways, in the sense that social characteristics are associated systematically with educational failure and success. These patterns are complex and multidimensional. The Equality and Human Rights Commission (2010), for instance, reports inequalities associated with, among other things, gender, ethnicity, sexual orientation, and – of particular significance for special needs education – disability. In particular, the Commission finds that inequalities in educational outcomes are 'strongly associated with socio-economic background' (Equality and Human Rights Commission, 2010, p. 300). The Commission is not alone in reaching this conclusion. A recent review of the research evidence for the RSA paints the following gloomy picture:

> British children's educational attainment is overwhelmingly linked to parental occupation, income, and qualifications. Marked differences become apparent during early childhood with regard to readiness for school. By the age of three, poor children have been assessed to be one year behind richer ones in terms of communication, and in some disadvantaged areas, up to 50% of children begin primary school without the necessary language and communication skills. As compulsory schooling progresses, educational inequalities continue to widen between children from poor families and those from more affluent backgrounds . . . Furthermore, these children are more likely to attend the lowest-performing schools in deprived areas. They are also disproportionately likely to have been in care, and/or have special educational needs. Although this is a widespread international phenomenon, and research has shown that social deprivation has a negative impact on educational attainment across all OECD countries, the UK has a particularly high degree of social segregation and is one of the nations with the most highly differentiated results among OECD countries.
>
> (Perry & Francis, 2010, p. 5; citations omitted)

In reality, the relationship between social background and educational outcomes is more complex than this account might suggest. The temptation is to posit a linear and deterministic relationship between the economic aspects of social background and educational outcomes – and, in particular, to see educational difficulties as 'caused' by economic deprivation. However, this is not the case. The economic aspects of families operate in interaction with, rather than separately from, other background factors such as ethnicity and gender (Cassen & Kingdon, 2007; Schools Analysis and Research Division, 2009). Moreover, social background comprises a wide range of factors at work in families and communities that are related to, but by no means identical to, economic background. Economically poor families may have much in common, but they also have different dynamics, come from different cultural traditions, and live in places where there are different educational and work opportunities. One useful way to understand these complexities is to view children as growing up in a series of interacting but distinct environments, each of which contains factors that help shape outcomes. Duckworth (2008, p. i), for instance, identifies four 'contexts' impacting on attainments at Key Stage 2:

- the *distal context* – background socio-demographic features, such as income, parental education, and so on
- the *proximal context* – parental support and parent–child relationships
- the *school–peer context* – the nature of the school and its population
- the *child context* – individual child ability, measured primarily in terms of prior attainment.

This conceptualization is important for understanding what can and cannot be done to equalize outcomes between children from different backgrounds and, specifically, to enable children from poorer backgrounds to do better. It is no doubt the case that countries with greater economic equality also tend to have more equal – and, arguably, better overall – educational and other outcomes (Wilkinson & Pickett, 2009). This means that there is a strong case for pursuing greater economic equality as a means of equalizing outcomes, but it does *not* mean that nothing can be done until the conditions are ripe for radical social change (Dyson et al., 2010). On the contrary, there are multiple factors in different contexts that it may be more feasible to change – such as, for instance, how parents support their children's learning, the skills and knowledge thatr children acquire before they enter the school system, and the quality of education the child experiences.

In this respect, Duckworth's analysis of the relative influence of different contexts on educational outcomes is illuminating. She finds that the child's prior attainment and background socio-demographic factors are more powerful than (though associated with) the proximal context of parental support, and much more powerful than the school–peer context. This last finding is initially somewhat surprising. Schools of course make an enormous contribution to what children know and can do. However, they do little to disturb the relationship between educational outcomes and the inequalities that children bring with them from their backgrounds. Indeed, if anything, inequalities seem to increase over most of the school years, albeit with some narrowing of these increased gaps between ages 14 and 16 (Goodman, Sibieta, & Washbrook, 2009). The explanation would seem to be that improving the overall quality of schools – which has been the focus of much policy in England over recent years – benefits all students in more or less the same way, and that efforts to 'narrow the gap' (DCSF/IDeA/LGA, 2007) between more and less advantaged groups have only limited impacts. Reviewing the evidence in this field, the school effectiveness researcher Daniel Muijs concludes that interventions within the school and classroom can never be more than part of the answer in the search for more equal outcomes:

> . . . even if we found all the factors that make schools more or less effective, we would still not be able to affect more than 30 percent of the variance in pupils' outcomes. It has therefore become increasingly clear that a narrow focus on the school as an institution will not be sufficient to enable work on more equitable

educational outcomes to progress . . . Interventions will need to impact more directly on pupils' environment and life chances. Work with the community is essential, if expectations are to be raised and social and cultural capacity built, as is work on health and socio-psychological inhibitors.

(Muijs, 2010, p. 89)

Special educational needs and educational inequalities

Special needs education is, of course, one of the major interventions available within schools for generating more equal outcomes. As the Audit Commission reported some time ago, the special needs system in England embraces one in five students and directs an additional 15 per cent of spending on schools towards these students, in addition to what many of them receive through their mainstream provision (Audit Commission, 2002). Moreover, it is clear that social background factors play a large part in determining who receives special needs provision. As Perry and Francis (2010) point out, children from poorer backgrounds are disproportionately likely not only to achieve less well at school, but also to find themselves in some form of special needs education. In fact, children entitled to free school meals are two to three times more likely than their more advantaged peers to be identified as having special educational needs, and the imbalance is even more marked for types of need that are defined socially rather than by means of objective measures of functioning (Lindsay, Pather, & Strand, 2006; Schools Analysis and Research Division, 2009). Moreover, the tendency for children from poorer backgrounds to be identified as having special educational needs is just one aspect of the wider phenomenon of 'disproportionality', whereby groups of students defined by their social characteristics are particularly likely to enter special needs provision. So, for instance, boys from a African-Caribbean background are much more likely to be identified in this way than are girls or students from Chinese backgrounds (Dyson & Gallannaugh, 2008; Lindsay et al., 2006).

As has long been recognized, therefore, special needs education does not respond only – or even largely – to children who happen to experience difficulties in school because of their idiosyncratic characteristics. It also responds to large numbers of students who experience difficulties for reasons that are related systematically to their social backgrounds. Put another way, special needs education is a response to the educational consequences of social inequalities at least as much as it is a response to individual differences (Tomlinson, 1982). Strangely, however, this reality seems to have played little part in shaping the practices and procedures of the special needs system. This may well be because that system has its origins in provision for children with identified impairments and medical conditions (DES, 1978), and is therefore rooted deeply in notions of individual difference. Although the system in England long ago moved from a simple equation of disability with special education, it remains the case that having 'a disability which prevents or hinders them from making use of educational facilities of a kind generally provided' (Education Act 1996, section 312, cited in the Code of Practice (DfES, 2001b, p. 6)) is one of two broad criteria used to indicate that a school student has special educational needs. While the second criterion – having 'a significantly greater difficulty in learning than the majority of children of the same age' – does indeed enable the system to respond to learners whose difficulties are not associated with disability, the assumption appears to be that these difficulties are idiosyncratic in origin. There is, therefore, no indication in the definitions and criteria of the special needs system that difficulties might be associated with social inequalities (by contrast, for instance, with the 'at-risk' category used in the USA and elsewhere).

In this situation, the special needs system in England has, not surprisingly, concentrated its energies on identifying the idiosyncratic nature of the needs generated by students' disabilities or 'learning difficulties'. The system in England has, therefore, developed complex procedures for individual assessment, planning, and intervention. These procedures become increasingly intensified and individualized as the severity of children's difficulties increases (DfE, 2010b), but the focus remains on finding interventions that are directed at the individual student and deployed primarily in learning situations within the school and classroom. Recent proposals are likely to simplify these procedures, but the focus remains firmly on identifying children who need a 'tailored approach' to help them learn and on 'planning and delivering the right support' in schools and classrooms to enable identified students to learn (DfE, 2011b, p. 68). Much less attention is paid to non-individual and contextual factors in children's social backgrounds.

This might not matter if the interventions typically associated with special needs education were sufficiently powerful to overcome these social factors. However, there is little reason to believe that special needs provision is any more powerful than schools overall in this respect. It is certainly the case that well-designed and well-implemented special needs interventions enable children to do better than they might otherwise have done (Kavale, 2007; Mitchell, 2008). Overall, however, the special needs population lags behind its peers throughout the school years, and at best the gap is fluctuating rather than closing (Goodman et al., 2009). Studies from the USA suggest that, even when the movements of students in and out of provision during the school years are taken into account, there is no evidence that special needs education has a transformational as opposed to merely ameliorative effect for the population as a whole (Bielinski & Ysseldyke, 2000).

Beyond special needs education

Over three decades ago, Lewis and Vulliamy (1980) observed that the understandings and interventions available to special needs education are limited by:

> . . . an implicit theory that neglects the importance of social factors in the causation of 'special educational needs'. Many handicaps are obviously the result of psychological or medical factors, whether congenital or otherwise. Yet education is now, surely, recognised as one of those areas in which the organisational structures of schools, together with teachers' expectations and pedagogies can create massive learning and behaviour problems for pupils . . . [S]ocial factors external to the school must also be considered in any assessment of why pupils either exhibit learning difficulties or become disruptive in school.
>
> (Lewis & Vulliamy, 1980, p. 5)

Since that time, it is fair to say that some attention has been focused on the origin of children's difficulties in the structures and practices of ordinary schools, and the English school system now has a much wider range of strategies available to respond to these difficulties than it had in the 1970s and 1980s. Indeed, the current reform proposals, referred to above, make much of the importance of meeting children's difficulties through good teaching and high expectations rather than simply labelling students as having special needs (DfE, 2011b, p. 67). However, the second aspect of Lewis and Vulliamy's 'social factors' – those that are external to the school – have remained largely neglected. As a result, special needs education has failed to develop interventions that might be deployed in respect of these factors. Even the considerable soul-searching associated with the rhetoric of inclusive education seems to have resulted in efforts to improve and democratize school practices rather than to tackle disadvantaging factors in students' backgrounds (Dyson & Gallannaugh, 2007). At best, schools have relied on their separately organized and rather low-powered 'pastoral' systems for any means of intervening in children's lives beyond the classroom. These systems too, however, appear to have retained a focus on individual problems and personal development, with few means of changing the conditions under which students live (Best, 2002).

However, this is not the whole story, and particularly not in recent years. However little may have been achieved in practice, the question of how to tackle the link between social disadvantage and poor educational outcomes has periodically troubled policy-makers since at least the time of the Plowden Report in the 1960s (Central Advisory Council for Education (England), 1967). Most recently, the advent of a centre-left New Labour government in 1997 brought renewed interest in this issue and led to a series of developments that, I wish to suggest, have implications for the role of special needs education in the future.

Although there is undoubtedly much to criticize about New Labour's approach and achievements between 1997 and 2010, some significant steps were taken to recognize the links between children's educational outcomes and their social backgrounds. New Labour policy in this field developed under the umbrella concept of 'social exclusion', which was defined as:

> . . . a shorthand term for what can happen when people or areas suffer from a combination of linked problems such as unemployment, poor skills, low incomes, unfair discrimination, poor housing, high crime, bad health and family breakdown.
>
> (Social Exclusion Unit, 2004, p. 4)

This notion of 'linked problems' translated in terms of children's policy into the *Every Child Matters* agenda (DfES, 2004a) and the *Children's Plan* (DCSF, 2007). In brief, New Labour governments sought to respond to the complex, interacting problems that they believed some children faced by establishing integrated service structures and coherent frameworks that would allow all those involved in working with children to collaborate on a common strategy. In practice, this meant bringing local authority-led education and social care services together into unified children's services, and establishing children's trusts to coordinate the full range of services locally (DCSF, 2008b).

These developments had significant implications for how schools were able – and were expected – to respond to children's difficulties. They were, for instance, expected to pursue outcomes well beyond those traditionally associated with education, acquiring (in the Education and Inspections Act 2006) wide-ranging duties to promote the overall 'well-being' of their students and the 'cohesion' of the communities they served. To do this, they had access not only to the newly integrated service structures in the local authority, but increasingly to multi-disciplinary service teams operating on the ground – usually on an area basis (Cummings, Dyson, Jones, Laing, & Todd, 2011a). Moreover, they were first encouraged, and then expected, to offer students and their families and communities access to a range of 'extended services', in terms, among other things, of childcare, study support, easy access to specialist services, parenting support, and adult learning (DCSF, undated; DfES, 2005b). As the various strands of these initiatives emerged, they ultimately coalesced into a vision of a 'Twenty-first Century School'. This, the government declared would embody a focus on:

- maintaining high aspirations for all children and young people and providing **excellent personalised education and development** to ensure that all are able to progress and reach high standards;

- enabling schools to play a key role in **identifying and helping to address additional needs**, working at the centre of a system of early intervention and targeted support; and

- providing a **range of activities and opportunities to enrich the lives of children, families and the wider community**; and contributing to community objectives such as local cohesion, sustainability and regeneration.

(DCSF, 2008a, p. 6; original emphases)

It would be disingenuous to suggest that these initiatives transformed schools' roles and practices in any simple and unproblematic way. They were undoubtedly characterized by conceptual ambiguities and by significant problems of implementation (see, for instance, Cummings, Dyson, & Todd, 2011b; Dyson, Farrell, Kerr, & Mearns, 2009; Levitas, 2005). Moreover, New Labour governments resolutely refused to undertake a root and branch reform of special needs education so that its structures and practices could be aligned with the new situation (HM Government, 2006). Nonetheless, they did create a framework within which schools, often working with local authorities, could marshal responses to children's difficulties that were not confined to traditional special needs or pastoral interventions, and which took into account factors beyond the school and classroom that might be impacting on children's learning. The form these responses took have been widely documented, not least in work by me and my colleagues (see, for instance, Cummings et al., 2007, 2010, 2011a, 2011b; Dyson, Kerr, & Weiner, 2011). On the basis of these accounts, it is possible to identify three key features that mark schools' responses out from the traditional approaches characteristic of special needs education.

New personnel and partnerships

Special needs provision has traditionally relied on a well-established set of personnel and partnerships to deliver interventions, mainly in classroom settings. School personnel have been more or less specially trained teaching staff, supported increasingly in recent years by teaching assistants. Their work has been supplemented by partnerships with a range of services able to formulate and deliver specialist interventions and services. These have included local authority support-teaching teams, education psychology services, and some non-educational services in the health and social care domains. These services have typically been accessed through referral processes, which, like the special needs assessment system itself, have become increasingly complex and formalized as the degree of specialization and extent of support increase.

In the 'new' approaches, however, schools have begun to employ adults from a wide range of personal and professional backgrounds, able to deploy interventions well beyond the classroom (Edwards, Lunt, & Stamou, 2010). These include learning mentors, counsellors, school-based social workers, play and leisure activity leaders, and, most prominent of all, various types of family support worker. At the same time, schools have both intensified and extended their partnerships with other agencies. They may well also now be working with youth workers, police officers, behaviour specialists, housing specialists, therapists of various kinds, youth justice workers, and health workers. Moreover, these professionals may be based in the school, or form a team liaising closely with the school's in-house support workers.

The head teacher of one school that colleagues and I studied described this new model of provision as being about filling in 'the zone inbetween' (Cummings et al., 2007, p. 36), by which he meant the gap in provision between the traditional pastoral work of schools and the specialist services available only through referral. The new approaches, at best, allow interventions to be marshalled rapidly across a number of aspects of children's lives, so that, for instance, problems in the classroom, problems in family relationships, and problems in the material conditions under which families live can be addressed simultaneously. Moreover, they do this without necessarily involving formal referral processes with their inbuilt delays and rationing systems, and through a collaborative approach that has the potential to reduce inter-agency turf wars.

New leadership and governance structures

Special needs education has well-established, though hugely problematic, structures for managing and governing provision (see, for instance, Audit Commission, 2002; House of Commons Education and Skills Committee, 2007). Put simply, provision is led in schools by more or less well-trained and more or less specialist teachers (so-called 'SENCOs'), and is governed beyond the school by local authorities, which have the unenviable tasks of managing finite resources and ensuring that individual schools make their best efforts with challenging and resource-intensive students.

These structures are somewhat resistant to change because they are sustained by statutory and regulatory requirements. Nonetheless, the new approaches are either incorporating them into, or overlaying them with, structures that look very different.

Within the school, special needs provision typically becomes part of the much more wide-ranging effort to tackle children's difficulties described above, and therefore its leadership becomes part of management structures with much wider remits. This can either take the form of expanding the role of SENCOs so that they have an extended responsibility for all aspects of student support, or downgrading the role so that they become part of a multi-specialist team led by a more senior colleague. Beyond the school, provision has increasingly come to be governed on an area basis, with clusters of schools collaborating with each other, and with decision-making structures of various kinds at local level deciding on priorities and managing a pooled set of resources across institutions and agencies. The consequence is that special needs provision is, to varying degrees, ceasing to be managed as a separate system offering a limited range of interventions that are 'additional to or different from' what is available in the mainstream classroom. Instead, it is becoming part of a much more powerful and wide-ranging system for supporting students and working with their families and communities.

Changing the unit of intervention

Special needs education has traditionally been concerned with intervening in the learning difficulties (broadly understood) of individual students. Indeed, *individual* education plans and programmes are one of the salient features of special needs systems in England as in other countries. Many of the interventions that take place within what we are calling the 'new' approaches continue to be focused on individual students – though, as we have seen, across a much wider range of issues. However, there is also a tendency for the unit of intervention to be broadened from the child to the family, and from the family to the community and area.

It is therefore increasingly common for schools to have ways of working with families that include, but also go well beyond, inviting them to occasional planning meetings or encouraging them to help their child work on learning activities at home. The family support workers mentioned above tackle a wide range of family issues, ranging from managing children's behaviour to dealing with relationship breakdown and ensuring access to benefits and specialist support. Moreover, because schools increasingly work with agencies that have a community or area role, and – in some cases at least – with employers who help shape the local economy, they are able to intervene in community dynamics and cultures, and in the economic conditions under which their students live. In some places, indeed, the work of the school with students and their families is explicitly seen as part of a wide-ranging area regeneration strategy (see, for instance, Barnsley Metropolitan Borough Council, 2005; Knowsley Council, 2008; Rowley & Dyson, 2011). This means that, perhaps for the first time, schools are in a position to tackle not only the difficulties that their students present, but also the family, community, and area conditions out of which these difficulties arise.

What future for special needs education?

It is, of course, important not to romanticize these developments. Quite apart from the difficulties that arise as they are implemented, the specific form they currently take in England is very much associated with a policy regime that is now in the past.

The general election of 2010 removed New Labour from office and installed a Conservative–Liberal Democrat Coalition government that shows little enthusiasm for involving schools in wide-ranging approaches to tackle 'social exclusion'. It is likely, therefore, that at least some of the developments of the past decade will be eroded over the next few years. By way of contrast, efforts to align what schools can achieve within classrooms with interventions beyond the classroom are not simply the products of a particular, short-lived policy regime. Whenever and wherever the connection between educational outcomes and social background is taken seriously, recognizably similar initiatives tend to emerge (Cummings et al., 2011b). Of particular note in the USA, for instance, is the Harlem Children's Zone (The Harlem Children's Zone, 2009; Tough, 2008), which seeks to tackle the significant disadvantages experienced by children in one of the poorest parts of New York City by aligning improvements in the internal practices of schools with a coherent early-years to college educational offer, and a series of interventions in the conditions of the area and community under which children live.

It is this notion of carefully aligned, multi-strand strategies that has the most significant implications for the future of special needs education. The problem of the special needs system in England – and, it seems reasonable to suppose, in many other countries – is not that it has deployed the wrong interventions, or that it has had no positive impacts at all. It is its failure to take into account the broader social contexts – the 'world out there' – in which learners live and grow. However, the developments reported above show that this need not be the case. Schools can indeed become part of something much bigger than themselves, expanding their remit into the 'zone inbetween' their traditional concerns and those of other agencies, and aligning their work with the much more powerful social interventions that those other agencies can bring to bear.

When this happens, special needs education need no longer be conceptualized as the only intervention available for tackling the educational difficulties faced by large numbers of disadvantaged students. Instead, it can be seen as a contribution to an overarching strategy for tackling the link between social and educational disadvantage. In principle, this might mean expanding the special educator's role (as described above) and the blurring of the boundary between special educational need and other forms of 'additional' educational need, as has happened recently in Scotland and Wales (National Assembly for Wales, 2006; Scottish Executive, 2005). In this way, an extended form of special needs education can take the lead in developing the overarching strategy. However, we have learned in the past that attempts to 'redefine' (Bines, 1986) or 'rethink' (Dyson & Gains, 1993) special needs education, or even to 'do away with' it entirely (Galletley, 1976), tend to founder when they are driven by the missionary zeal of radical special educators intent on reforming their schools. Not only are schools much harder to change than the missionaries often suppose, but special needs provision itself is highly resilient in the face of efforts at reconstruction (Dyson & Millward, 2000).

It therefore seems to me that efforts to rethink special needs education have to be initiated and driven from outside that field. Broad, area-based strategies have to come first, and almost certainly have to be developed by school leaders and local decision-makers rather than by reconstructed special educators. Once these strategies are in place, and once they are aligned with flexible and high-quality mainstream educational provision, a more realistic appraisal can be made of how much special needs education and of what kind might be needed. My guess is that there will always be a need for well-designed interventions and support systems that are confined to the setting where learning takes place. If special needs education can supply these, it will continue to have a future. However, we almost certainly need less of it than we currently have, and what we have needs to be aligned much more carefully with the more powerful strategies to which it should contribute.

SECTION 2

This section builds on and extends the exploration of issues surrounding special educational needs and disability (SEND) by focusing on key discrete topics disclosed by educators, educationalists, and research in discussing practice, particularly in light of increased calls over the last 20 years that it should attend to the wider needs of the child or young person with SEND.

The implications of this holistic view are addressed. Chapter 5 considers the role of mental health and of therapeutic interventions in the educational setting. Chapter 6 is an exploration of what concepts such as self-esteem imply for a child's learning and development. Chapter 7 focuses attention on the notion of student participation in their learning and decisions made that affect them. Chapter 8 then considers how a child's behaviour can be seen to be a part of a wider set of relationships.

Finally, Chapter 9 brings both sections of the book together by drawing on the expertise of the contributing authors to create an 'ideal' school and classroom.

5

TERRY HANLEY, NEIL HUMPHREY AND CLARE LENNIE
The therapeutic classroom: challenging the 'mad, bad or sad' hypothesis

Introduction

Sabia, oh she's a 'self-harmer'!

Jack's just an angry kid and always will be.

Sophie's always over-emotional and crying in class.

These three statements are presented to get you thinking. Before continuing, just stop for a moment and consider what you make of them. Have you heard people utter such statements? Do you feel they are adequate summaries of some of the young people or children you come across in schools or communities across the UK?

We hope that this chapter will make you consider the complexities in navigating through the early years of life and possibly reconsider viewing these statements as appropriate conclusions. We begin by briefly considering our three young people a little further and relating back to thinking from the field of humanistic psychology. Then we consider commonplace strategies for supporting children and young people within the education system. We introduce interventions that are more systemic in their approach (i.e. working with a whole school or on a group level) before moving on to consider those that are being implemented in a more targeted way (i.e. one-to-one therapy). Finally, we pull together a few of the threads that have been discussed in this chapter and reflect on the potential implications for educators.

Sabia, Jack and Sophie (and Ishmael)

Returning to the statements introduced at the beginning of this chapter, we find some relatively common sentiments within large educational establishments. In an environment that can see hundreds or thousands of children or young people being managed within one geographical location every day, there are likely to be shorthand interpretations and explanations for the behaviour of pupils (see Riddick, Chapter 2). This may be inevitable and unavoidable, although we would also argue that when relationships break down there is often a need acknowledge this for what it is, notably a crude stereotype based on limited understanding of the full situation. We propose that the humanistic psychology movement may have something to offer here. This movement developed during the 1960s in response to the growing disillusionment with the major psychological forces of psychodynamic and behavioural theories. It also provides a core value base for the profession of counselling psychology, which we will discuss later in this chapter (Strawbridge & Woolfe, 2010). So what is it? Let us reflect on the key postulates of the movement as a starting point (Bugental, 1964):

- Human beings, as human, supersede the sum of their parts. They cannot be reduced to components.
- Human beings have their existence in a uniquely human context, as well as in a cosmic ecology.
- Human beings are awake and aware of being aware; that is, they are conscious. Human consciousness always includes an awareness of oneself in the context of other people.
- Human beings have some choice and, with that, responsibility.
- Human beings are intentional, aim at goals, are aware that they cause future events, and seek meaning, value and creativity.

Although there may be terms that turn you off within these statements, we hope that you get the sense of the ethics of the humanistic movement. These concepts can be boiled down to reflect that humans are incredibly complex and ultimately unique, that they move towards meaningful growth, and that they have choice in life situations (Gillon, 2007).

Following on from the very brief introduction to humanistic psychology presented above, let us consider each of the statements we initially presented in turn. First, we have Sabia:

Sabia, oh she's a 'self-harmer'!

In this instance, the teacher is defining Sabia by a complex set of behaviours and the shorthand term 'self-harmer' is used. Such sentiments can be perceived as insensitive and very dismissive. Furthermore, they ignore the uniqueness to the situation that has led this young person to hurt herself. Saying 'Sabia is a person who self-harms' would therefore be one way of acknowledging the person rather the behaviour in the first instance. Such issues with language arise around conceptualizations of well-being all the time. For instance, John might be depressed, or Tim could be a schizophrenic, but what do we mean? Although these terms acknowledge diagnoses of mental health conditions, these are culturally defined criteria for summarizing groupings of behaviours. They fluctuate and can be manipulated (see, for example, Rosenham's (1973) fascinating seminal study 'On being sane in insane places'), and they often do not give us an insight into the origins of the behaviour. Essentially, they are shorthand for a broader set of issues and we would encourage looking beyond such terms when making decisions that are important to the lives of young people. Just because individuals do things that are difficult to comprehend does not make them mad.

We next consider both Jack and Sophie together to reflect two sides to a similar difficulty:

Jack's just an angry kid and always will be.

Sophie's always over-emotional and crying in class.

Here we have the stereotypical naughty boy (bad) and emotional girl (sad). Once again we would like to highlight the complexity that is likely to lie behind each of these behaviours. We also reflect on the optimism embedded in humanistic psychology and the determination for individuals to strive towards 'actualization' (Maslow, 1954). In both of these statements, the teachers in question insinuate that the behaviours will be ongoing and, in the case of Jack, they will never change. Such sentiments go against the notion that humans will strive towards meaningful growth and can change given the right environment in which to do so. Sophie may therefore be unhappy at this point in time, but this is likely to be in response to certain experiences in her life. Jack's anger may also be seen in a similar light. Here the message would be not to give up on individuals even if they present with enduring difficulties.

Finally, we introduce Ishmael to make one final point:

It was Ishmael's decision to set the firework off in school and so he should be excluded permanently.

This is an incredibly complex statement. Ishmael could be viewed as another bad young man who made an active choice to do something dangerous. It is the choice that he had on which we focus here. As noted earlier, humanistic psychology believes that individuals generally have choice, which includes the choice to end one's life. The complexity arises when we consider the pressures around individuals when making decisions. For instance, was Ishmael under pressure from peers to set the firework off? Would he have suffered greater harm if he had not done so at that particular time? It is without doubt a complex arena and to use an expression of *Guardian* columnist Ben Goldacre (who revels in reporting the limitations and misrepresentations of research findings), 'I think you'll find it's a bit more complicated than that.'

Now that we have introduced a number of young people, and the way they may be perceived to be 'mad', 'bad' or 'sad', we move on to discuss the types of therapeutic support for school aged children. We begin by outlining the place that mental health has within school settings before discussing the types of school-based strategy that are becoming increasingly prevalent. We then introduce more targeted therapeutic interventions and consider these within the major paradigms of practice.

The broader mental health of schools/mental health in schools

Schools are complex social systems, not least with regard to the roles that are allocated to supporting the emotional and social needs of the learner. Job titles such as teaching assistant, special educational needs coordinator, learning mentor, and behaviour support tutor are commonplace in classrooms in the UK alongside whole-school initiatives in aiming to promote the more holistic aspects of education. Furthermore, outside the school environment, referrals can be made to the likes of educational, clinical, and counselling psychologists, all of whom may have somewhat different aims and goals regarding the specific interventions offered.

As outlined above, the discourses around a child's presenting issues can often be labelling, pathologizing, and negative in connotation, rather than focusing on the more positive aspects of the child's presenting behaviour. One way of responding to this has been for schools to utilize a positive educational practice (PEP) framework to promote the positive aspects of a school's planning. The ultimate hope for such an approach is that positive whole-school-based initiatives will trickle down to individual staff and student well-being and resilience by intentionally cultivating a whole-school plan. The underpinnings of the PEP framework come primarily from the work of Martin Seligman and positive psychology, the major focus of which is to facilitate flourishing lives that promote organizational as well as individual well-being. The four main aims of this approach are

1   To generate positive emotions (e.g. satisfaction, pride, belonging, and enjoyment).
2   The development of mastery and competence through a skills-based approach.
3   Engagement with school by working with strengths.
4   The development of a sense of meaning and purpose.

Positive educational practice frameworks have clear links with the ethos of humanistic psychology articulated above, particularly those claiming that human beings are awake and aware, have choice and responsibility, and are intentional (Bugental, 1964).

As part of this move away from the traditional, rationalist view of education and the purpose of schooling, there has been an increasing emphasis on a holistic view of learners. Much of this paradigm shift took place under New Labour, which introduced a wide range of educational initiatives, many of which had a direct focus on fostering resilience, social and emotional skills, or well-being more broadly. Examples include:

* *National Healthy School Standard* (DfEE, 1999)
* *Every Child Matters* (DfES, 2004a)
* *Social and Emotional Aspects of Learning (SEAL)* (DCSF, 2005)
* *Targeted Mental Health in Schools* (DCSF, 2008d)
* *Achievement for All* (DfE, 2010a)

Schools are seen to be among the most important and effective agencies for promoting the mental health of children and young people (Squires, 2010; Weare & Markham, 2005), and the introduction of the policies listed above reflects this viewpoint. Furthermore, under New Labour schools were expected to be more accountable for this aspect of their provision, with the introduction of 'personal development and well-being' as one of the strands used in school inspections by the Office for Standards in Education (Ofsted) during the period in which these policies were rolled out.

Although we have subsequently changed government in England, the early indications are that the current Coalition administration is equally focused on promoting well-being.

The enactment of policies such as those listed above has tended to reflect a model of whole-school preventative work, supported by more targeted interventions for learners at particular risk of or already experiencing social and emotional difficulties. The 'social and emotional aspects of learning' (SEAL) programme is a good example of this. SEAL is a comprehensive, whole-school approach to promoting the social and emotional skills that are thought to underpin effective learning, positive behaviour, regular attendance, and emotional well-being (DfES, 2005a, 2006a). It is reported to be in use in around 90 per cent of primary schools and 70 per cent of secondary schools in England (Humphrey, Lendrum, & Wigelsworth, 2010).

The SEAL programme is somewhat unique in relation to the broader literature on approaches to social and emotional learning in that it is envisaged as a loose enabling framework for school improvement (Weare, 2010) rather than a structured 'package' that is applied to schools. Schools are actively encouraged to explore different approaches to implementation that support identified school improvement priorities rather than following a single model, meaning that they can tailor it to their own circumstances and needs. In a sense, this means that SEAL is essentially what individual schools make of it rather than being a single, consistently definable entity. It was conceptualized in this manner to avoid the lack of ownership and sustainability that might be associated with the more 'top-down', prescribed approach that is taken in the USA.

There are three 'waves of intervention' to the delivery of SEAL (see Figure 5.1). The first wave of SEAL delivery centres on whole-school development work designed to create the ethos and climate within which social and emotional skills can be most

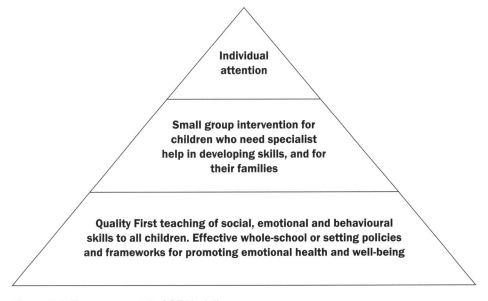

Figure 5.1 The wave model of SEAL delivery

effectively promoted. The second wave of SEAL involves small group interventions for children who are thought to require additional support to develop their social and emotional skills (DfES, 2005a, 2006a). The final wave of the SEAL programme involves one-to-one intervention with children who have not benefited from the whole-school and small group provision in a given school, and are thought to be at risk of or experiencing mental health difficulties. In many schools, this element has been delivered under the remit of the *Targeted Mental Health in Schools* (TAMHS) initiative, using some of the kinds of intervention outlined in the next section of this chapter. The TAMHS initiative, like SEAL, is presented as an enabling framework rather than a 'package' of materials to be delivered. Among the key elements of the TAMHS approach are the promotion of evidence-informed practice and the facilitation of effective inter-agency collaboration (DCSF, 2008d).

The SEAL programme is designed to promote the development and application to learning of social and emotional skills that have been classified under the five domains proposed in Goleman's (1995) model of emotional intelligence. These are:

- self-awareness
- self-regulation (managing feelings)
- motivation
- empathy
- social skill.

At the school level, SEAL is characterized by the following principles:

- Implementation of SEAL is underpinned by clear planning focused on improving standards, behaviour, and attendance.
- Building a school ethos that provides a climate and conditions to promote social and emotional skills.
- All children are provided with planned opportunities to develop and enhance social and emotional skills.
- Adults are provided with opportunities to enhance their own social and emotional skills.
- Staff recognize the significance of social and emotional skills to effective learning and to the well-being of pupils.
- Pupils who would benefit from additional support have access to small group work.
- There is a strong commitment to involving pupils in all aspects of school life.
- There is a strong commitment to working positively with parents and carers.
- The school engages well with other schools, the local community, wider services and local agencies (National Strategies SEAL Priorities, 2009–2011).

Research on the effectiveness of the various strands of the SEAL programme has produced mixed results (for a review, see Humphrey, forthcoming). The programme itself has also not been without criticism (e.g. Craig, 2007; Ecclestone & Hayes, 2008). However, despite this controversy, schools have embraced it enthusiastically as a framework through which to develop provision in a way that considers the personal, social, and emotional growth of learners rather than just their academic prowess.

Supporting young people: what targeted interventions are on offer?

The sections above outline some of the work undertaken on a whole-school level to promote mental health. However, often a more targeted individual therapeutic intervention is the preferred option. Currently, it is estimated that there are over 500 different types of therapy related to work with children (Kazdin, 2000) and a variety of factors need to be considered in choosing the appropriate form of intervention. The child's developmental stage is central to understanding their cognitive, self-reflective, and social capacities, which are drawn on to a greater and lesser extent in different modalities of working. For example, very young children are limited in their ability to self-reflect, or indeed to use language to describe and discuss their reflections and experience. This will impact on the work undertaken and may perhaps result more in behavioural approaches that focus on explaining behaviour and supporting parenting skills. Alongside this, the child's social context is central; children are rarely in a position to change their social context and their family or immediate social groupings will be an important filter through which experience is construed (Downey, 2003). Due to this, some would argue that counselling the child individually detracts from understanding the important influences and dynamics that are exerted on the child by the family, therefore espousing a family therapy approach. Others would suggest that working with the family dilutes the potential for personal issues to be fully explored and worked with.

In the sections below, we outline the three major paradigms of individual therapeutic practice. Then we discuss practical ways of integrating approaches of therapy and refer directly to the literature on school-based therapy. We reflect briefly on the historical developments of each model, the potential applications for work with younger client groups, and the research related to such work. We also direct the reader where possible to useful literature and resources for work with young people using these three approaches.

Behavioural and cognitive approaches

Behavioural approaches concentrate on behaviour and the consequences of action, rather than what is going on mentally in terms of thought processes. Based on the work of Pavlov, the basic premise is that if a stimulus such as food is paired often enough with a neutral stimulus, such as a bell, then an animal or human will eventually respond to the bell by salivating. This new response, learned through association, might generalize to other sounds outside of the laboratory and can find its application in work with, for example, phobias, where usually neutral stimuli become associated with a stressful experience.

Following from this work, Skinner and Watson proposed that the consequences of our actions are important in determining the likelihood of them reappearing. Put simply, if something pleasant happens after we have behaved in a certain way, we are likely to do it again. We also repeat our behaviours if we avoid something unpleasant happening, but our behaviour will cease if something unpleasant does happen. It could be argued that Jack's angry behaviour, outlined above, is maintained through the attention that he receives from those around him, thus reinforcing and maintaining his actions. Although there is no need for particular insight in this intervention, the model does require for the child to be motivated to engage in therapy with a level of self-control and awareness of their presenting behaviour. Due to their emphasis on measurable behaviour, there is more empirical research on these approaches. For example, systematic desensitization, where clients are gradually exposed to their feared stimulus while pairing it with relaxation, has generally been found to be helpful with simple phobias in young children (Ollendick & King, 1998).

In cognitive behavioural therapy (CBT), there is still an emphasis on behavioural components, as outlined above, but with a further focus on the cognitions associated with maintaining behaviours (Squires, 2001, 2002). Cognitive behavioural therapy is not just concerned with fixing problems but also with the achievement of a happier life with discrete and meaningful goals, rather than broad-based 'therapy'. The here-and-now is emphasized rather than the past, with a realistic and positive reframing of negative thoughts to reduce negative emotions. Developing competency in helpful and reality-based thinking as a buffer to future problems is emphasized, with scheduling of pleasant activities accompanied by mood monitoring, identification and review of success experienced, and the development of problem-solving competencies (Karwoski et al., 2006).

Although perhaps better suited to older children when their cognitive and linguistic skills become more sophisticated, CBT has been reported to be helpful with a number of child psychological problems such as generalized anxiety (Silverman et al., 1999), depressive disorders (Lewinsohn & Clarke, 1999), and social phobias (Spence, Donovan, & Brechman-Toussaint, 2000). Cognitive behavioural therapy for such disorders has five components (Albano & Kendall, 2002):

- *Psycho-educational*: providing corrective information about anxiety and feared stimuli.
- *Somatic management skills training*: targeting autonomic arousal and physiological responses.
- *Cognitive restructuring skills*: focusing on identifying maladaptive thoughts and teaching coping-focused thinking
- *Exposure methods*: involving graduated and controlled exposure to feared situations.
- *Relapse prevention plans*: focusing on consolidating and generalizing treatment gains.

In addition, specialized manuals offer resources to the practitioner in relation to some of the core concepts of CBT (see, for example, Stallard, 2002, 2005).

Psychodynamic approaches

Psychodynamic approaches base themselves around the importance of the relationship in therapy, viewing this as the primary instrument for change in terms of interpretation, personal insight, and awareness. Due to its focus on the relationship, and where this has been damaged early in life, it is likely that the child will have to have a number of sessions at the start of therapy to develop an enduring and transportable sense of the relationship (Downey, 2003).

The roots of psychodynamic therapy lie in the work of Sigmund Freud and the psychosexual stages of development and theory of personality. Underlying each of these are Freud's ideas of ego functions, defence mechanisms, and superego formulation. This was later developed in the USA to incorporate thinking about attachment, object relations, and the importance of working with parents through the work of Bowlby and Klein. With its emphasis once again on higher level cognitive and linguistic skills, it is unlikely that this way of working would be appropriate for younger children. However, attributes of children who may benefit from psychodynamic psychotherapy include (Delgado, 2008):

- conflict-free areas of functioning
- relate to and communicate well with others at an age-appropriate level
- demonstrate interest in school or hobbies
- awareness of symptoms and wish for change
- ability to use metaphor
- affect (emotional) stability with some capacity for ambivalence.

In working psychodynamically with children, therapists need to be aware of issues of transference where the child might respond to the counsellor as if their mother or some other significant person in their life. Such transference can be worked through in a session by bringing it to the child's awareness. Counter-transference occurs where the counsellor responds to the child's transference unconsciously, as if he or she were that significant other, and this needs to be owned and worked through by the therapist. Such underlying unconscious conflicts form the basis for psychodynamic work but it is important to remember that these can be tapped into by methods other than the verbal, such as through play (Harrison, 2003).

It is unusual for long-term 'pure' psychodynamic work to be offered in a school largely due to practical limitations of the setting. For instance, immediately being returned to the school environment after a session might not be appropriate, thus mediating the necessary boundaries needed in this type of work is important. Broader psychodynamic interventions offered are likely to help in understanding the dynamics that arise between pupils, family members, school staff, and issues of parenting. Wilson (2004) and Youell (2006) describe how dysfunctional attachment and relationship patterns in the family can arise in the school setting and are able to be worked through by bringing them into conscious awareness through deep understanding, so impacting on the new relationships into which the child enters (Lanyado & Horne, 2009).

Person-centred approaches

The main founder of this methos was Carl Rogers who, disenchanted with more mainstream approaches to psychology and the objectivist stance of behaviourism, believed that human beings had an innate need for respect and understanding. His ideas are still central to professional work where human growth is seen as central and his core principles can be summarized as follows (Cain, 2002):

- Emphasizing the central role and importance of the counselling relationship itself as a significant factor in promoting change.

- Describing 'the person' as resourceful and tending towards actualization of potential.

- Emphasizing and developing the central roles of listening and empathy in counselling and other relationships.

- Using the term 'client' rather than 'patient' to signify respect for the person coming for help and to acknowledge his or her dignity.

- Making sound recordings of counselling interviews and using them to learn about the counselling process.

- Engaging in scientific research and encouraging others to do so.

- Making the counselling process more democratic and encouraging non-psychologists and non-medical people to become counsellors.

Essentially, this approach to helping is concerned with enabling the counsellor or helper to help the client to access their own wisdom in a way that acknowledges that the client knows best. For this reason, this approach is often referred to as client-centred or non-directive counselling. In work particularly with children, the counsellor–child relationship is fundamental and provides a link between the child's inner world and the counsellor. It must therefore be exclusive, safe, authentic, confidential (subject to limits), non-intrusive, and purposeful (Geldard & Geldard, 2009).

Common factors: practitioner skills

Given that the research findings indicate that there is little difference in the effectiveness of different types of therapeutic intervention (e.g. Wampold, 2001), alternative ideas of working with young people come from integrative or pluralistic approaches. For example, an integrative stance would draw on a number of models as appropriate to the child's need, the goals of which may differ as the child progresses. Concepts from person-centred counselling may be drawn on as the child tells their story and later ideas from cognitive behavioural therapy might be used in working with maladaptive thoughts, options, and choices. Finally, as the child experiments with new behaviours, these are evaluated from a behavioural perspective. These methods promote a different model of change, drawing on different types of intervention with the ultimate goal of making the child feel better (Geldard & Geldard, 2009).

A pluralistic approach meanwhile would emphasize the common factors of therapy and, rather than looking to apply a model of working to a client's problem, would advocate that the business of counselling can be broken down into key tasks that then draw on appropriate methods of intervention to reach the young person's goal (Cooper & McLeod, 2007, 2011). When young people were asked about what they found most helpful about counselling, the key themes to emerge were being listened to and understood by someone who was non-judgemental (Cooper, 2006a). Thus, the findings of this work closely mirror the tenets of person-centred counselling. However, questions and advice were also found to be useful alongside skills that may have formed part of the work, for example relaxation exercises drawing on cognitive and behavioural components. Finally, when questioned about what young people feel they do in therapy, commonly they report being given the opportunity to talk, to reflect on their issues, and to explore alternative ways of behaving and responding. Such findings emphasize that one approach to therapy may not be best and that young people value a wide variety of interventions.

Therapy in schools

As is evident above, there are numerous brands of therapy that young people may encounter within school settings. Therapeutic professionals therefore come into play and 'counsellors' and to a lesser extent 'psychotherapists' have become increasingly common within schools. A survey of schools in England and Wales reported that approximately 75 per cent had a counsellor to whom students had access (Jenkins & Polat, 2005). Furthermore, within the UK, this trend seems to be on the increase and counsellors are now being introduced into all secondary schools in Wales (Welsh Assembly Government, 2008), most primary schools in Northern Ireland (Northern Ireland Office, 2006), and there is a target for providing counselling in Scottish schools and communities by 2015 (Public Health Institute of Scotland, 2003). In addition, some children can access therapeutic support from educational psychologists (Atkinson, Bragg, Squires, Muscutt, & Wasilewski, 2011; Squires & Dunsmuir, 2011). Such a groundswell of provision makes therapy in school settings a major component in supporting the well-being of young people within the UK.

To date, there is limited research to inform the practice of school-based therapy services. A meta-analysis of 30 audit and evaluation studies in the UK reported an incredibly positive effect of such services (Cooper, 2009). This reflected the experiences of approximately 10,830 clients, with counsellors reporting to work from a person-centred or integrative therapeutic approach. In summary, the meta-analysis noted that 'School-based counselling appears to be of considerable benefit to young people in the UK' (Cooper, 2009, p. 137). Such a finding is also complemented by the developing, but limited, amount of qualitative research in this area. Research studies have examined individuals' perceptions and experiences of counselling (Chan & Quinn, 2009; Cooper, 2006b; Pattison et al., 2007; Quinn & Chan, 2009) and reflect that young people often perceive counselling to be helpful, and that stakeholders (e.g. young people, parents, and teachers) are generally satisfied with such provision.

There are weaknesses to the arguments posed by advocates of school-based counselling. As noted earlier in this chapter, there are a wide variety of targeted psychological interventions on offer to young people and, in much the same way that the SEAL initiative could be challenged because of its flexibility, school-based counselling could be viewed in a similar light. For instance, in the meta-analysis above, a further conclusion was that 'there is a need for the findings to be verified through controlled trials' (Cooper, 2009, p. 137). Thus, the uncontrolled nature of the environment, and the overall messiness of the data collected, compromised the conclusions that could be drawn from the study to some degree. As a response to this, a randomized controlled trial exploring the impact of humanistic school-based counselling was piloted (Cooper et al., 2010). This showed little difference between the control group and those who had attended counselling. The limited success of the intervention was primarily attributed to weaknesses within the design of the project and follow-up trials are ongoing at the time of writing. In providing a view from outside the UK, another meta-analysis exploring school-based counselling and psychotherapy within the USA reported more modest findings (Baskin et al., 2010). This meta-analysis addressed 107 studies, predominantly cognitive behavioural in nature, and displayed an overall moderate effect size for the interventions. The authors found that adolescents benefited more than children from therapeutic work, and that work with licensed professionals was better than therapeutic interventions offered by paraprofessionals (e.g. teachers).

Studies that use routinely generated practice-based data highlight some of the complexities of attempting to evaluate therapeutic work in school settings. Although Cooper's (2009) meta-analysis used this type of data and produced positive findings, it noted a large remission rate among those that took part. A study that used a more systematic approach at collating routine evaluation data displayed yet more complexities (Hanley, Sefi, & Lennie, 2011). In this study, eight young people within therapy were tracked on a session-by-session basis using several common psychological measures. The patterns of well-being scores collected displayed eight incredibly varied therapeutic journeys and highlight some of the potential perils of presenting studies that use pre- and post-therapy measures in a way that suggests they tell the whole story.

School-based counselling and psychotherapy is a complex area, and one that researchers are only scratching the surface of understanding at present. Some of these complexities might be partly explained by the messiness of naturalistic school environments; the turbulent nature of adolescence itself (e.g. consider the lives of Sabia, Jack, Sophie, and Ishmael introduced earlier in this chapter); the actual nature of what therapeutic services for young people offer (e.g. 'are counselling services providing supportive interventions and containment of development complexities or are they aiming to reduce psychopathological symptoms?'); and limitations in the methodologies utilized to evaluate such work.

Summary and implications for educators

In this chapter, we have covered a great deal of territory. This is very much a starting point for anyone interested in the therapeutic developments that have taken place within schools but we hope that the content proves informative and gives people a sense of the broad array of therapeutic interventions already being adopted within educational establishments. For some, developments in this area will be viewed as a step in the wrong direction – after all, isn't school about teaching young people curriculum-based topics?

For others, these developments will complement curriculum teaching and support young people in coping with the demands of everyday life (during school and beyond). It should be relatively clear that we primarily fall into the latter category and would advocate many of the strategies discussed above. From our perspective, Sabia, Jack, Sophie, and Ishmael are young people growing up in an incredibly complex environment. They will be subjected to numerous challenges and encounter many opportunities. With these eventualities in mind, for some learning how to become resilient enough to ride the knocks and make best use of those opportunities that do head their way is a relatively simple process. For others, however, additional support of the kinds introduced above may offer young people the opportunity to develop skills that enable them to live life more fruitful lives. Two reflective questions you might ask yourself are:

- Should therapeutic services be integrated into a school ethos or kept separate?
- Do schools have a duty of care to support young people around mental health issues?

Having noted the increasing emotional support now available within schools throughout the UK, we should also note that this is not unconditional and blinkered. Support has to be provided for an informed purpose and be backed by a sound rationale. As evident within this chapter, many of these interventions have been evaluated (or are continually being examined) and this body of knowledge can help inform decisions about provision. Caution is warranted here, however, as research is often wielded like a wooden club in the hands of a small toddler by policy-makers. Schools are messy environments and the young people within them inevitably have complicated lives. Evaluation projects are often rife with complexities and confounding variables. Provision based on such work therefore should become more accurately framed as research-informed rather than evidence based. Some questions to consider include:

- Should mental health interventions in schools have an observable positive impact on educational performance (individual or school based)?
- Should mental health interventions in schools have an observable positive impact on the adult lives of recipients?

Those of you who are more research-oriented in your thinking may want to also consider:

- Is it possible to conduct a randomized controlled trial exploring psychological interventions in a school setting?
- Is small-scale qualitative research sufficient to influence a school's policy on social and emotional aspects of learning?

We do not provide any answers here but hope that we have conveyed some of the complexities in the ways in which research may be used to inform therapeutic interventions in the classroom.

6

NEIL HUMPHREY
Self-esteem in the classroom

Introduction

The aim of this chapter is to demonstrate the role played by children's developing self-perceptions in determining their behaviour, relationships, and learning in the classroom. It begins with a discussion of issues relating to definition and conceptualization of the 'self-system' (with a particular focus on self-esteem), followed by a brief outline of its development and influences during the school years. The attention then turns to what research evidence tells us about self-esteem in relation to learners with special educational needs – with specific reference to those children with dyslexia. The chapter concludes by considering implications for educational practice.

Terms like 'self-concept', 'self-confidence', 'self-perceptions', and in particular 'self-esteem' have become part of our everyday educational lexicon in recent decades. This mirrors a broader pattern at a societal level, where our obsession with the self-system is reflected in a burgeoning self-help industry (one need only look in the self-help and/or popular psychology section of any major bookstore for evidence of this) and the popularity of television programmes that either explicitly or implicitly deal with issues of self-esteem and self-confidence (e.g. 'How to Look Good Naked'). Positive self-perceptions have come to be viewed as a panacea, with proponents claiming that if we just taught people how to value themselves more, they would also become happier, more productive, experience greater interpersonal success, and lead healthier lifestyles (Baumeister, Campbell, Krueger, & Vohs, 2003). Similarly, many of the problems in modern society have been blamed on an apparent epidemic of low self-esteem:

> I cannot think of a single psychological difficulty – from anxiety and depression, to fear of intimacy or of success, to alcohol or drug abuse, to underachievement at school or at work, to spouse battering or child molestation, to sexual dysfunctions or emotional immaturity, to suicide or crimes of violence – that is not traceable to poor self-esteem.
>
> (Branden, 1994, p. xv)

Critics have been quick to point out the flaws in such claims (e.g. Baumeister et al., 2003; Hewitt, 1998) and the debate continues, particularly in relation to questions around the means and value of actively attempting to enhance self-esteem (Carlock, 1999; O'Mara, Marsh, Craven, & Debus, 2006). This issue is brought sharply into focus in education, where recent years have seen a move away from traditional, rationalist views of schooling, towards an active consideration of 'the whole child' – within which the notion of self-esteem is central.

Definitions and key principles

Despite more than 100 years of attention and thousands of published studies, fundamental issues regarding self-esteem remain poorly understood.

(Leary, 1999, p. 33)

As self-concept, self-esteem, and so on are part of our folk language, the definition and conceptualization of these terms are rarely given adequate attention (O'Mara et al., 2006). This appears somewhat out of step with the importance ascribed to them in educational and psychological circles (if, for example, self-esteem is so vital to adaptive functioning of the individual, surely we need to agree on what it is before we devise the means to enhance it). The definition I provide below draws on the work of influential modern theorists such as Herbert Marsh (1985) and Susan Harter (1999), in addition to historical figures such as William James (1890).

To understand the basic self-system (see Figure 6.1), we need to think about three interrelated components. *Self-concept* is the descriptive component of the self; for instance, 'I am bad at maths.' The *ideal self* is aspirational in nature, and refers to how we would like to be; for instance, 'It is important for me to be good at maths.' Finally, *self-esteem* is the affective component of the self-system, denoting a sense of worth attached to oneself based on the relationship between our self-concept and ideal self;

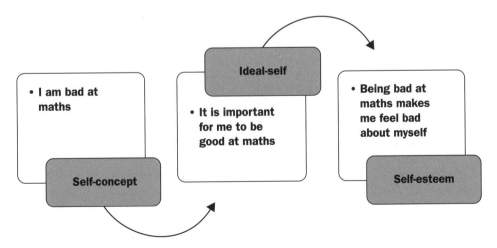

Figure 6.1 A basic overview of the self-system

for instance, 'Being bad at maths makes me feel bad about myself.' It is important to note that as self-esteem is contingent on values ascribed in the ideal self, it is therefore highly idiosyncratic in nature (Crocker & Wolfe, 2001). Using the example above, my poor maths self-concept is more likely to impact on my sense of self-esteem because being good at maths is part of my personal aspirations and values.

There are several key principles that characterize the self-system. First, it is important to note that although at a basic level it is possible to talk about an individual's global sense of self (e.g. 'She has really high self-esteem'), modern theory and research has demonstrated that it is in fact multidimensional and hierarchical in nature (Marsh, 1985; Shavelson, Hubner, & Stanton, 1976) (see Figure 6.2). Thus, it is possible for an individual to have a positive sense of self in some areas (e.g. social relationships) and not others (e.g. school). The extent to which these different self-perceptions contribute to the individual's overall self-esteem is contingent on the values imposed by the ideal self.

The second key principle of the self-system is that it is formed entirely through social experience. Our self-perceptions take shape through our interactions with other people. The feedback others provide, both explicitly through the things they say, and implicitly through their behaviour towards us, provide us with a 'mirror' for understanding ourselves (coined the 'looking glass self' by Cooley, 1902). Feedback that is presented regularly and consistently is most likely to take hold in the self-concept, particularly if it is congruent with our existing beliefs about ourselves. For example, research has demonstrated that individuals suffering from depression are more likely to filter out positive feedback and focus on negative feedback they receive from other people because this is more consistent with their perception of themselves (Swann, Wenzlaff, Krull, & Pelham, 1992).

The third key principle of the self-system is a natural corollary of the second. In practical terms, it would be impossible for us to incorporate *all* of the feedback we receive from *everyone* with whom we interact. There would simply be too much information to absorb, and much of it would be inconsistent in nature. Thus, we have a tendency to focus mainly on the feedback we receive from key figures in our lives – known as our 'significant others' (Burns, 1982). Our significant others can and do change over the lifespan, but in childhood and adolescence it has been argued that

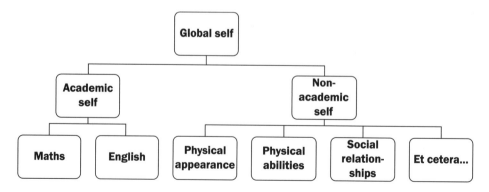

Figure 6.2 The multidimensional and hierarchical self-system

parents (Greenberg, Siegel, & Leitch, 1983), teachers (Humphrey, 2003), and peers (Harris, 1999) are the most influential. Given the increasingly important role it plays in our lives, it is also possible to think of the media as significant others. Consider, for example, the influence of television and magazines in influencing the physical self-esteem of young people (Berel & Irving, 1998).

The final key principle of the self-system is that it influences (and is influenced by) other psychosocial constructs. Of particular relevance given the overall focus of this chapter are *attributional style* and *locus of control*. Attributions are the causal explanations we give for events. For example, a pupil might attribute his or her success on an exam to the amount of hard work and revision he or she did. Attributions for events can be broadly categorized as internal/external ('I passed the test because I'm clever' versus 'I passed the test because my teacher is excellent') and stable/unstable ('I passed the test because English is easy' versus 'I passed the test because I did a lot of work') (Humphrey, 2002). Locus of control is closely linked to attributional style, as it describes the extent to which individuals believe that they can influence the things that happen to them. Attributional style and locus of control relate directly to the self-system. So, for example, individuals with a negative view of themselves may be more likely to make attributions that reinforce that view; for example, a child with negative academic self-perceptions may attribute a success at school to external factors.

Summary of key points

- The key components of the self-system are the self-concept (descriptive), ideal self (aspirational), and self-esteem (evaluative).
- The self-system is multidimensional and hierarchical in nature.
- The self-system is formed entirely through social experience.
- Some individuals – known as significant others – are particularly important in the development and maintenance of our sense of self.

The development of self-perceptions during childhood and adolescence

Our sense of self is in a state of constant development and refinement during childhood and adolescence. A key early milestone is the development of *self-awareness*, which typically occurs at around 12 months (Berger, 2005). Before this, young infants make no distinction between themselves and the external environment. Once they become self-aware, however, a line begins to be drawn between the internal world of 'self' and the external world. A classic experiment that demonstrates this emergent sense of self involves drawing a small mark on an infant's forehead, before holding them up in front of a mirror. Those who look in the mirror and finger the mark have clearly recognized themselves – a key hallmark of self-awareness (Lewis & Brooks-Gunn, 1978).

Self-perceptions during childhood and adolescence follow the trajectory of cognitive, linguistic, and social development. That is, a young child's sense of self reflects how they think, how they talk, and their knowledge of and interactions with other people. Susan Harter's (1999) excellent *The Construction of Self* provides a useful overview, replicated in Table 6.1.

Table 6.1 The development of self-perceptions during childhood and adolescence

Period of development	What do children focus on when they describe themselves?	How is this self-perception organized or structured?	How accurate are these self-perceptions?	What comparisons do children make when describing themselves?	How sensitive are they to what other people say or do?
Very early childhood	Concrete, observable characteristics	Isolated representations that lack coherence; all-or-none thinking	Unrealistically positive; cannot distinguish real from ideal self	No direct comparisons	Anticipation of adult standards (e.g. praise, criticism)
Early to middle childhood	Elaborated attributes; focus on specific competencies	Basic links between representations, typically using opposites; all-or-none thinking	Typically positive; inaccuracies persist	Temporal comparisons with self when younger; comparisons with age mates to determine fairness	Initial integration of others' opinions; others' standards of behaviour become internalized to regulate behaviour
Middle to late childhood	Trait labels that focus on abilities and interpersonal characteristics; general evaluation of self-worth	Higher order generalizations that cover several behaviours	Both positive and negative evaluations, with greater accuracy	Social comparison for purpose of self-evaluation	Full internalization of others' standards and opinions
Early adolescence	Social skills, attributes linked to social appeal	Inter-coordination of trait labels into single abstractions	Positive attributes at one point in time, negative at another, leading to inaccurate over-generalizations	Social comparison continues, although less overt	Attention to different standards and opinions in different relational contexts
Middle adolescence	Further differentiation of attributes associated with different roles and contexts	Initial links between single abstractions, often with opposing attributes; cognitive conflict and concern over which reflects true self	Simultaneous recognition of positive and negative attributes; instability, leading to confusion and inaccuracies	Comparison with significant others in different relational contexts	Awareness of potential conflict of differing standards and opinions of others, leading to confusion; imaginary audience

Adapted from The construction of self, Harter S (1999). Copyright Guilford Press. Reprinted with permission of Guilford Press.

There are several patterns and trends that are worthy of note here. First, the way in which children describe themselves and what they focus on when doing so becomes increasingly sophisticated throughout childhood and adolescence. They begin in early childhood with very basic descriptions of things that can be observed (e.g. 'I'm a big girl'), but by adolescence are focusing on a whole range of attributes, many of which are abstract, and are even describing themselves in different ways depending on role and context. The structure of their self-perceptions follows a similar pattern, becoming increasingly differentiated and complex, particularly during adolescence. Finally, the role played by other people, both in terms of the comparisons children make and the influence of others in determining their self-perceptions, also increases greatly throughout the school years.

In terms of overall self-esteem, research has suggested that it is typically high during childhood, but drops during adolescence (Robins & Trzesniewski, 2005); this is perhaps unsurprising given the changes in the nature of self-evaluation between these two periods of development. The stability of self-esteem also appears to change, increasing from childhood through to adolescence (Robins & Trzesniewski, 2005). There are, of course, implications within the above for educators. First, the feedback (both implicit and explicit) provided by teachers and other school staff becomes more important as children get older. One key example of the importance of teacher behaviour is seen in the research on the use of different types of praise on children's self-perceptions. Mueller and Dweck (1998) tested the commonly held belief that praise for ability has beneficial effects on motivation. Contrary to expectations, they found that praising children for intelligence made them highly performance oriented and thus extremely vulnerable to the effects of subsequent setbacks; consistently telling children that they are intelligent when they pass tasks may therefore have negative long-term consequences for self-esteem. It has been suggested that praise for effort may be more beneficial (Kamins & Dweck, 1999; Mueller & Dweck, 1998; Owens, 1997), but this may be difficult to instil in an education system where the emphasis is increasingly placed on achievement (Humphrey, Charlton, & Newton, 2004).

Second, the increasing use of social comparisons in determining children's self-perceptions has important consequences when we consider issues around educational placement and setting (for instance, whether children are taught in classes streamed by ability, or whether learners with special educational needs are taught in mainstream or specialist settings) – an area of research that has led to the development of the 'Big Fish Little Pond' effect (Marsh, 1987). The peer group also becomes more influential as children progress through school, both as a source of feedback to be integrated into the self-system, and in helping to determine the values and aspirations of children, particularly in relation to their attitudes to education and their academic self-perceptions (Humphrey et al., 2004).

Systemic factors may also be considered influential here though. The ethos and atmosphere within a given school – in particular the implicit messages about values, respect, and diversity that are infused in everyday school life – can have a powerful effect on individual learners. A final consideration in considering the development of self-perceptions in the educational context is the proposed reciprocal relationship between self-esteem and academic achievement (Marsh & Yeung, 1997). This model, validated in a number of rigorous studies, proposes that children's academic self-perceptions influence their later academic achievement, which subsequently serve to modify later academic self-perceptions (for example, a learner with a negative academic self-concept is more likely to do poorly in a school test; this outcome subsequently serves to reinforce – and even exacerbate – their view of themselves as being a weak learner).

Summary of key points

- Children's self-perceptions reflect their cognitive, linguistic, and social development.

- Their self-perceptions become increasingly complex and differentiated as they get older.

- Teachers and peers take on increasingly important roles through childhood and adolescence.

- Self-esteem is generally higher in childhood than adolescence, but is less stable.

- These developmental trends have implications for education, including placement and setting.

Self-esteem among learners with special educational needs – the case example of dyslexia

Consistent with the overall theme of this book, our attention now turns to children and young people with special educational needs and disabilities (SEND). I use the specific case example of learners with dyslexia for several reasons. First, such children form a significant proportion of the overall population of those with SEN (Humphrey & Squires, 2010). Second, the educational difficulties typically experienced by learners with dyslexia have powerful implications for the self-system given the developmental pathway and influences outlined above. Perhaps because of this, they are also the SEND group for whom the most research on self-esteem exists, meaning a more detailed picture is possible.

Research focusing on self-esteem among learners with dyslexia is a relatively new phenomenon; indeed, it is only in the last two decades that studies have begun to emerge that have examined this topic. However, it is an issue that – anecdotally at least – has long been a concern of educators, pupils, and their families. In the mid-1990s, two books were published that gave an indication of the educational experiences of children with dyslexia and the subsequent effects on their personal, social, and emotional development (including their self-esteem). The first of these, Edwards' (1984) *The Scars of Dyslexia*, explored retrospective accounts of the schooling experience of eight adults diagnosed with dyslexia. Edwards found that the negative emotional consequences of these individuals' experiences as dyslexic learners in the education system were still evident even in adulthood. The second book, Riddick's (1996) *Living with Dyslexia*, presented the findings of a research project that explored the experience of being a dyslexic learner from the perspective of the children and young people themselves, and their families. In a similar vein to Edwards (1984), Riddick found that children with dyslexia felt 'disappointed, frustrated, ashamed, fed up, sad, depressed, angry and embarrassed by their difficulties' (Riddick, 1996, p. 60). Moreover, around half of the children interviewed had been teased about their difficulties, and many recalled upsetting experiences involving teachers who did not acknowledge their difficulties (for example, attributing their poor literacy to a lack of effort).

As useful and influential as these two books were, it was important to establish whether the findings indicated above in relation to the effects of dyslexia on children's self-esteem could be borne out using other research methodologies. My doctoral research, carried out from 1998 to 2001, sought to explore the relationship between dyslexia and a range of related psychosocial constructs including self-perceptions, attributions for academic success and failure, and personal constructs. In the course of the project, I compared these among children with dyslexia attending mainstream schools, those with dyslexia attending mainstream schools that included specially resourced units for supporting pupils with specific learning difficulties (SpLD), and a comparison group of children attending mainstream schools with no identified SEN. In addition, I interviewed the children in the two dyslexic groups about their experiences of schooling and perceptions of themselves. The main findings of this research were that the presence of dyslexia produced marked effects on the self-concept and self-esteem of children, although this was more apparent in those attending mainstream schools than those in SpLD units (Humphrey & Mullins, 2002a). These differences were particularly evident in the data from measures that looked specifically at aspects of pupils' academic self-perceptions (Humphrey, 2002). Such findings are consistent with the aforementioned Big Fish Little Pond Effect theory (Marsh, 1987).

In terms of attributional style, when academically successful dyslexic pupils were significantly more likely to attribute their outcome to external factors (meaning that such events did not serve to facilitate a positive sense of self). In contrast, pupils without dyslexia were significantly more likely to attribute their outcome to external factors when failing academically, thus preserving their self-esteem (Humphrey & Mullins, 2002b). The qualitative data revealed that children with dyslexia felt isolated and excluded in their schools, and that, in a similar vein to the findings of Riddick (1996), up to half were regularly teased or bullied (Humphrey & Mullins, 2002a). Many of the students also defined dyslexia in a negative way – for example, saying that it meant that they had something wrong with their brains (Humphrey, 2002). Interestingly, they had developed such understandings from things that parents and/or teachers had told them.

It is important not to be too pessimistic here. Burden and Burdett (2005) have challenged the notion that dyslexia is to be *automatically* associated with low self-esteem, and reminds us of the need to consider the circumstances and contexts in which pupils with dyslexia can come to view themselves as capable, motivated learners (however, it is important to note that this research was based on data from pupils in specialist settings – the Big Fish Little Pond Effect theory would predict a more positive sense of self among learners in such contexts). Furthermore, research by Riddick (2000) and colleagues (Riddick, Wolfe, & Lumsden, 2003) present the labelling of a child as dyslexic as a potentially positive step for the individual involved, as it offers a legitimate explanation for the genuine difficulties that they are experiencing. This also serves as a counterpoint to negative attributions made by peers or teachers, such as the disabling labels 'thick' or 'lazy' (Edwards, 1984; Humphrey, 2002). As such, diagnosis can enable a positive 'reframing' of previous educational experiences (Gerber, Reiff, & Ginsberg, 1996).

One crucial factor in determining how dyslexia influences self-esteem appears to be the strategies adopted by individual learners as they integrate the notion of dyslexia into their identities. In an attempt to explain these processes, David Armstrong and I interviewed students to see how they reacted to their diagnosis, and how this reaction informed their understanding of self and identity, in addition to their educational experiences (Armstrong & Humphrey, 2009). We developed a 'resistance–accommodation' model, which suggests that reactions to dyslexia can be conceptualized along a continuum of resistance and accommodation. Resistance is characterized by an unwillingness or inability to accept and integrate the status of dyslexia into the individual's sense of self, often as a result of the stigma associated with the term. Resistance to diagnosis was often associated with negative connotations of the term 'dyslexia'. Accommodation, by contrast, is characterized by successful integration of an individual's dyslexic status into his or her notion of self, and is typically associated with a more positive view of dyslexia, construed as a *difference* rather than a *deficit*.

Summary of key points

- Dyslexia provides a powerful case of the effects of living with special educational needs on learners' self-perceptions.

- Research findings reinforce the importance of significant others (e.g. teachers, peers) in determining children's self-esteem – the effects of bullying and teasing, for example, can last through to adulthood.

- Educational setting is also important – the evidence supports Marsh's (1987) Big Fish Little Pond Effect theory about the nature of social comparisons that children make in schools.

- Dyslexia does not automatically yield negative consequences for children's self-esteem – much appears to depend on the experiences of individuals and the way in which they integrate their dyslexic status into their identity.

Implications for educators

In this final section, my aim is to draw out the practical implications of the theory and research outlined earlier in the chapter. Although these implications may be particularly relevant in considering the needs of pupils who experience difficulties during their schooling (such as those with dyslexia), they are also broadly applicable to all children and young people as part of fostering an inclusive classroom ethos.

Promoting a positive construction of differences between learners

This is a basic starting point. A common theme in explanatory discussions of the relationship between SEND (in this case, dyslexia) and self-esteem is the extent to which affected pupils develop a negative or positive construction of the label that is applied to them. The explanations offered by parents and professionals are crucial here. Consider, for example, the way in which the concept of dyslexia was introduced to some of the children in my aforementioned research (Humphrey, 2002), who subsequently came to believe that *there was something inherently 'wrong' with them*. Thus, it is important that explanations given to children and young people with special educational needs by parents and professionals focus on 'differences' rather than 'deficits'. Crucially, this needs to be supported by a classroom ethos in which differences and diversity of all kinds (e.g. educational, linguistic, ethnic, religious) are acknowledged and celebrated (for research into how some teachers in primary school settings achieve this, see Humphrey et al., 2006).

Early identification of special educational needs

Research outlined earlier in this chapter has suggested that a crucial factor in deter-mining the impact of special educational needs on the self-esteem of dyslexic children is the extent to which they are able to successfully integrate the label applied to them into their sense of self (see, for example, Armstrong & Humphrey, 2009). It therefore stands to reason that identification and assessment of special educational needs should be carried out as early as possible. First, and most basically, earlier identification gives learners more time to integrate the notion of their special needs into their identity (which is more malleable in the early years). Second, through the explanatory mech-anism offered by the label of, for example, 'dyslexia', learners are able to reframe their educational experiences in a positive way (e.g. 'I struggle with reading because I am dyslexic and learn in a different way to other pupils' rather than 'I struggle with reading because I am lazy or stupid'). Third, earlier identification can inform develop-ments in provision, such that individual differences between learners can be better accommodated.

Use of praise and feedback

The praise and feedback given by school staff is a key source of information for children in terms of their developing self-perceptions. Teachers are significant others and the things they say hold sway in the minds of their pupils. Consider, for example, that many of the children in my dyslexia research had come to believe that they were 'lazy' or 'stupid' because this is what they had been told by school staff (Humphrey, 2003; Humphrey, 2002). Thus, the feedback given – both implicit and explicit – must be given careful consideration, particularly among learners with special educational needs, whose self-perceptions may be more fragile than those of other children.

In terms of praise, as discussed above, research suggests that a 'blind' approach to praise (wherein children are praised regardless of whether they earned it or not) is not beneficial. Furthermore, praise for ability may have unexpected negative conse-quences. Praise for effort may therefore be the most powerful motivator (Kamins & Dweck, 1999; Mueller & Dweck, 1998; Owens, 1997; Squires, 1996), and is an adap-tive approach in terms of attributional style and locus of control, since effort is always under a given pupil's control.

Promoting positive peer relationships

The research discussed above highlighted the role of the peer group in influencing pupils' self-perceptions. In the case example of dyslexia, the peer group were often a source of negative feedback through bullying and teasing (Humphrey, 2002; Riddick, 1996). Intervention at this level is therefore an important consideration in attempts to facilitate a sense of belonging and acceptance among students with special educational needs. It has been suggested that this can be achieved through the development of peer support systems that encourage a sense of community within school. Thus, students are actively encouraged to seek help from each other and to offer help when it is needed, to share rather than compete for friends, and to act as advocates for those who they feel have been treated unfairly. Such practices, alongside an overarching humanistic school climate that is characterized by preference for democratic procedures, high degrees of interaction, and a respect for individual dignity, have been shown to foster positive self-perceptions in students (Hoge, Smit, & Hanson, 1990).

Dedication

This chapter is dedicated to Dr Pat Mullins, my PhD supervisor, who sadly passed away in 2009. She was a fantastic tutor and a constant source of inspiration and motivation during my study of dyslexia and self-esteem.

7

HAZEL LAWSON AND CAROLYN PURSLOW
The democratic classroom

Introduction

This chapter takes a broad view of democracy as 'an idea about how people might live together' (Beane, 2005, p. 8) and focuses on the notion of the *democratic classroom*. We ask the following questions: How can the classroom be a democratic place and space? In what ways can this be developed especially with regard to those pupils designated as having special educational needs?

The chapter commences with an analysis of democratic principles and how these might relate to the classroom. The concepts of *participation*, *person-centredness*, *recognition of difference*, and *social learning*, in particular, are examined. Three practical examples are then provided, each of which exemplifies aspects of democratic classroom practice and poses additional dilemmas and challenges. Finally, we examine these examples in the context of wider democratic principles.

Democratic schools and democratic education

The word *democracy* has Greek derivations meaning 'rule of the people'. It is, of course, generally used to refer to a system of political governance associated with equality, in terms of each person's vote having equal weight and people being regarded as equal before the law. It is also used in broader ways, and here we take Beane's (2005, p. 8) definition of democracy as 'an idea about how people might live together' and his proposition of two core principles that underpin democracy: '(1) that people have a fundamental right to human dignity and (2) that people have a responsibility to care about the common good and the dignity and welfare of others' (pp. 8–9).

Literature around democratic schooling (frequently from the USA, e.g. Apple & Beane, 1995; Beane, 2005) presents a picture of schools where pupils have the right to decide how, what, when, where, and with whom they learn and have an equal say to staff in decision-making about how the school is run (European Democratic Education Community, 2011). Regular democratic meetings involving one-person, one-vote are often a fundamental feature of these schools. In the UK, democratic schooling is commonly associated with 'alternative' education and 'free' schools such as Summerhill (Neill, 1962). (The UK Coalition government of 2010 has recently introduced a very different form of 'free schools' where the freedom is associated with freedom from some government and most local authority control (DfE, 2010e).) However, 'the spaces for [such]alternative versions of educational provision are now heavily constrained' (Stronach & Piper, 2008, p. 6). Curriculum content is heavily regulated through national curricula, and pedagogy is directed and controlled to some extent (in England, for example, through the notions of lesson structure as once advocated in the primary and secondary strategies (DfES, 2006b) and the expectations of Ofsted). Schools are also subject to considerable accountability through inspection regimes, standards, targets, and league tables. In these ways, despite a common-sense rhetoric of democracy, schools generally may be considered to be more autocratic than democratic (see Squires, Chapter 1).

Although democratic schooling is associated with whole-school structures, governance, and ethos, democratic education is also interpreted and enacted in other ways, for example, as the promotion of student voice and pupil participation (Fielding, 2004), as pedagogical teacher–student relationships (Rogers, 1969), as cooperative learning (Johnson & Johnson, 1996), and as programmes of citizenship education preparing pupils for adult citizenship (Print, 2007). This chapter takes some of these aspects and explores them in greater depth, with particular reference to children and young people designated as having special educational needs (SEN).

The democratic classroom

If we apply Beane's (2005) core democratic principles (personal human dignity and responsibility for caring about the common good) to the classroom, what do these look like? How can they be emphasized, practised, and incorporated into the classroom setting?

Human dignity: participation and person-centredness

For Beane, the right to human dignity includes rights of participation, the right to think for oneself, and to pursue personal aspirations. In relation to these rights, here we focus on two concepts: participation and person-centredness.

Participation of, and consultation with, children and young people in many areas of educational decision-making and practice is now commonplace. There is increasing professional and statutory commitment to this (DCSF, 2008e), building on the UN Convention on the Rights of the Child (UNCRC) (United Nations, 1989), particularly articles 12 and 13, that children's opinions must be listened to seriously in all matters that affect their lives and that children have the right to express themselves freely and to access information, subject to prevailing laws. Participation takes many forms, including choice-making and involvement in decision-making within the classroom, pupil consultations, and formal systems-related participation (e.g. individual education plan processes, school councils, students on governing bodies). Different levels of participation are often referred to – from being informed, taking part, and being consulted, to collaborating as reciprocal partners (Hart, 1992; May, 2004; Rudd, Colligan, & Naik, 2006). This emphasis on pupil participation is particularly apparent for children designated as having SEN and/or disabilities (DCSF/DH, 2007; DfES, 2001b, 2001c).

Lawson (2010), however, referring to the participation of children and young people with significant learning difficulties, cautions about the possibilities and dangers of professional-led participation. Participation may be limited to particular voices and may be conditional – if you are old enough, mature enough, understand enough (May, 2004). There is also a danger that the practice of participation becomes a tokenistic and bureaucratic operation, just a 'symbolic gesture' (Allan, 2008) where student consultations, for example, are not acted on. Lundy (2007, p. 931) argues that involvement of pupils in decision-making should not be seen as 'an option which is in the gift of adults' but as 'a legal imperative which is the right of the child'.

Person-centredness has also gained prominence recently, especially when working with pupils designated as having severe or profound and multiple learning difficulties. It has transferred into the education context from health and social care services, often regarded as being initiated in the UK by the Department of Health's *Valuing People* White Paper, which set out the need for 'person centred planning' for adults with learning disabilities (DH, 2001). A person-centred approach is described as discovering and acting on what is important to a person from their own perspective, taking account their wishes and aspirations (DH, 2001, 2009). Within education, this approach is intended to support everyone to be the best that they can be, to ensure everyone has a voice, and to put the young person at the heart of any planning and decision-making process (Devon Children's Trust Partnership, undated). A distinction needs to be made between *person-centred planning*, and the range of tools provided and promoted for this process (see, for example, DH, 2010), and a more general and all-encompassing *person-centred approach*. It is not as simple as training people how to complete a person-centred plan and hope that the plan will be enough to make a difference in people's lives (Routledge, Sanderson, & Greig, 2002). A person-centred approach involves some notion of risk (Methven, 2009; Neill et al., 2009; Seale & Nind, 2010). In education, this requires that professionals and other adults relinquish some control, empower young people, and allow questions to be asked to which they – the adults – might not know the answer. Such an approach seems to demand a cultural shift. Any consideration in particular of 'who's in control' appears to be problematic, acting as a barrier to progress in this area (see, for example, Dowling, Manthorpe, & Cowley, 2007).

Caring about the common good: recognition of difference and social learning

Beane's second principle of caring about the common good and the dignity of others concerns ways of working and being with others. It might include cooperative learning approaches, the way in which groups are organized, how difference is recognized and catered for, and an emphasis on social learning activities. Here, we explore two specific aspects: recognition of difference and the social context in learning.

Recognition of difference
A communitarian approach to democracy, aiming for consensus, might bridge or smooth out difference, treating everyone the same. Treating everyone the same,

however, does not equate with equitability. The principle of *equality* assumes fairness by the uniform application of the same expectation, standard or treatment, whereas the principle of *equity* acknowledges that applying the same treatment or standard to everyone without regard to individual differences does not necessarily have an equitable impact on everyone (Creamer, 2000). It is argued that the *acknowledgment of difference* is fundamental for democracy (Wildemeersch & Vandenabeele, 2007).

There is a tension and predicament here, particularly when working with children designated as having SEN, which Norwich (2007) refers to as a dilemma of difference. If we recognize difference so as to understand and cater for individual needs and interests, we may also perpetuate a view of difference as having lower status and less value; if we recognize difference, it can lead to different provision, but this provision might be stigmatized and devalued. If we do not recognize difference, however, we may not provide adequately for individuals. An example might be the provision of additional support for children in the form of withdrawal classes.

The social context in learning

A number of different learning theories emphasize the importance of a 'social' aspect in learning. Bandura's (1977) social learning theory, for example, argues that people learn through observing and modelling *other people's* behaviour. Vygotsky's (1978) social constructivist theory of learning proposes that *social interaction* plays a fundamental role in the process of cognitive development and that social learning precedes individual development. And, for Lave and Wenger's (1990) situated learning theory, *interaction* and *collaboration with others* are regarded as essential components: learners become involved in a 'community of practice'. The last two learning theories promote a social learning context where pupils play an active role, learning through interaction and collaboration with others – other learners and the teacher. The roles of the teacher and learner may be shifted in such contexts, such that teachers act as facilitators rather than transmitters of knowledge – again a possible cultural shift.

The social context of learning might also involve consideration of, and closer collaboration with, local communities. For young people with SEND in specialist settings, the notion of local community can be particularly problematic. Often such schools serve a wide geographical area and children and young people have lengthy journeys to travel to school. Children and young people with SEND (special educational needs and disability) frequently have limited engagement with social networks outside of school (Lewis et al., 2007), and the school community, whether mainstream or special, may be of greater importance than any geographical community. Indeed, in a study about citizenship education, pupils viewed school as the main social and participative community in their lives (Ireland, Kerr, Lopes, Nelson, & Cleaver, 2006). This further highlights the importance of participation within the school context.

In terms of democracy, Dewey (1966) emphasizes its social conception and contextual dimensions. He suggests that we only become who we are through participation in a social medium and that we must participate in democratic life to be a democratic person (Biesta, 2007). How, then, can such ideas and concepts be incorporated in the classroom?

Democracy in the classroom: practical examples

The following examples illustrate some features of democratic classroom practice and raise further issues, challenges, and tensions. They practically exemplify the concepts of pupil participation, person-centred practices, recognition of difference, and social aspects of learning with children and young people designated as having SEND. Each example does not necessarily reflect a single concept or element. Rather, the different aspects overlap within the examples. Permission for inclusion of the different stories has been gained and the names of pupils have been changed.

One of the authors, Carolyn, works at a school for pupils aged 3–19 years defined as having severe or profound and multiple learning difficulties. All of the children and young people have a Statement of Special Educational Need and each Statement is reviewed annually through a meeting of different stakeholders, including the pupil, parents, teachers, and other professionals working with the child or young person. In the first two examples, Carolyn describes the development of person-centred annual review processes at the school.

Example 1: Person-centred annual reviews

The school used to rely on a mainstream knowledge curriculum based on the National Curriculum, although massively differentiated. Therapy and skills for independence were squeezed into the gaps. A few years ago, two members of staff trained as facilitators of *person-centred reviews* (Sanderson, 2000) and started to facilitate these new forms of annual review meetings for students and their families. This was a significantly different approach from the traditional education-based reviews. For me, it was a revelation and the start of a new journey.

Regarding the *Valuing People* (DH, 2001) person-centred planning initiative, Routledge et al. (2002, p. 3) suggested that we would have 'to pay serious attention to advice on implementation, key issues of context and complementary activities' to successfully support effective change in this area. The issue of context seems particularly crucial and appears to relate to bringing the person-centred approach out of the meeting room and closer to everyday life. It also applies at many levels, including the immediate context (where and with whom one works, lives, socializes), as well as the wider cultural and social contexts in which the young people live.

The soundscape of the traditional review meeting was dominated by 'education' talk led by a senior member of staff, usually the head teacher or special educational needs coordinator (SENCo). The new style review is facilitated, not 'chaired', and the young person and their family are expected to be equal participants with the range of professionals from education, social care, and health. The social lives, home life, and health of the young person are considered as well as their education.

The review process, which is built on a particular model for transition reviews (Sanderson, 2000), includes 'what we like and admire' about the young person and asks 'What is important to you now?' and 'What is important to you for the future?', so that their dreams and aspirations start to frame and inform the discussions about them and their future. We also ask family members and others who work with the young person, 'What is important for the young person to keep them healthy and safe?' This gathering of information helps to establish the context for planning a young person's learning journey and, for older students, their transition from school to college, work, and so on.

The annual review is not thought of as an isolated event within the year of the child, but is placed within the annual teaching and learning cycle. Preparation for the review, developing skills for participation and engagement in the review, and the influence of the review action plan all impact on curriculum planning for each child or young person. Analysis of information gathered from the reviews forms the basis for the whole-school development plan.

We had thus begun the journey towards a reform of the school curriculum and the pedagogy that underpinned our practice and we were about to pay further serious attention to Routledge and colleagues' (2002) key issues of context and complementary activities. We were expecting young people to participate in their reviews, so we had to consider the skills required and where to place that skill development within the curriculum. If we were expecting our young people to make meaningful choices and decisions about their future beyond school, then we had to explore the process of decision-making and look at how we could prepare and enable our young people to express their preferences, make their choices, and participate in this decision-making.

Thinking about the development of these participation skills led to provision of different opportunities across the Key Stages and across the curriculum and, at times, involved tailoring to individual children. For example, in a lower Key Stage 2 class, children explored fairy tales. Over the term, the 'Little Red Riding Hood' story area was developed in the classroom with large two-dimensional characters on the wall, a costume box, a bed, and a basket. Within the structured environment of a known story, the children then explored new versions of the story and were offered opportunities to choose alternative endings. In another example, an upper Key Stage 2 class chose an animal from a selection offered to use as a trigger for story-making. The teacher worked with individual children or small groups to devise a story based on taking the animal for a walk. The teacher started the story with: 'Once upon a time there was a giraffe. The giraffe's name was . . .'. Someone named the giraffe Rachel. The teacher said: 'Rachel went for a walk' and she handed the giraffe to one of the pupils and opened the classroom door. The teacher followed the child with a camera as she travelled, taking photos of the giraffe as it was placed or dropped in different places. The teacher's commentary was limited to 'What happened next?', recording any words or sounds the pupil made. When the giraffe's journey was over, the teacher downloaded the photos and sat with the storyteller and another two children to add text to the photos. She recorded their words verbatim. The story was printed and bound into a book.

The changes to the annual review processes clearly led to changes across the school in terms of person-centredness and participation. The next example illustrates how an individual pupil's views might be established and presented for an annual review.

Example 2: Information-gathering and making choices

Michael has been at the school since he was 5 years old. He is now 19 and in his final year of schooling. He was living with foster carers but has been living in a residential home for a year. He is a healthy young man, physically able and very sociable. Michael has been chosen because he is very articulate and it would be easy to assume when you meet him that it would be quite straightforward to gather information about what is important to him and what he would like to do when he leaves school. However, we have observed over the last year that when Michael is asked a question about how he is feeling or about what he likes, his answers can appear at odds with his behaviour. He uses verbal communication but it can mean the opposite of what he wants to say. As a result, his teacher Emma says: 'You must never take one clip or one moment of a student and pretend that's their voice.'

Emma described a series of conversations she had with Michael and talked about some of the methods she is using to gather information and evidence about him to support his transition from school. When asked 'What are the things you most like doing?', Michael replied: 'Gardening. Do you like gardening? I don't do I? Do I like gardening?' He answered her question with a series of questions. When he first joined her class, Emma used to take his group to work on the school allotment. Michael would never settle down to a task, he would disrupt the work of others, and throw things to distract people. Initially, Emma and her team thought it was a result of his transition to a new class, although these patterns of behaviour were uncommon in other lessons. Later in the year, the students in this class were given opportunities to make choices about their personal timetable. Each morning, options were laid out that included art project, preparing lunch, and work on the allotment. Emma said:

> We often talk about meaningful choices and decisions. In order to express a preference or make a meaningful choice, students should be informed and have some real or related experience of the available options and, when offered a choice, they may need a verbal or visual prompt to recall their experience.

Emma and her team gather information about their students' preferences and choice-making all the time – writing notes, taking photos, asking questions, observing behaviour. Michael is in his second year in Emma's class and he has not chosen to go to the allotment for more than 12 months. At his last transition meeting, a support worker from Michael's home said that she thought a part-time course at the local horticultural college might be a good idea for Michael when he left school. He could join one of the other clients from the home. Emma said that she did not think he liked gardening, but when the support worker asked Michael directly, Michael said he did like gardening and he was going to horticultural college.

Emma believes that it is vital to prepare young people for their review because what they say in such circumstances may be coloured by being with people not normally in school, by being in a different room or just by leaving their lesson to attend a meeting. Michael is anxious to please people and avoid conflict and he is supported in his meetings and reviews by taking in photo posters and showing a PowerPoint presentation of himself at work and leisure in and around school. Michael likes photographs and they are very important to him; we know this because he chooses to look through them and he always has spare photos in his school drawer and in his bag. Most of the photographs are of his family, including previous foster carers, which suggests that they continue to be important to him. Emma worked alongside Michael to prepare posters with some of these photographs of family, carers, and school, helping him to portray his life story and express some of what he values. From a great number of photos she asked him to choose his favourites and place them under different headings, such as 'My family', 'My foster carers', 'My home', and 'My school'. She repeated the exercise six times over two months and found that he remained consistent in his choices. She then used the photos to trigger conversations about what was important to him now and what his dreams were for the future. The posters and records of conversations provided some evidence of what might be considered 'non-negotiable' for Michael, including his dislike and fear of cats, dogs, and other small animals and his love of cooking. The information framed and informed the discussions about his future beyond school, placing him at the centre. At a later transition meeting, Emma was able to talk with Michael and the support worker from his home and share the information she had gathered over the year about what was 'important to' Michael. As a result, and as one aspect of the next phase in his life, the horticultural college option was changed to a 'Skills for Living' course that would involve cooking.

Example 3: Social learning and recognition of difference – 'The Fashion and Beauty Group'

We have noted that the social context of learning involves consideration of, and close collaboration with, other learners and local communities, and we have recognized the challenge this presents for young people placed in special schools – they are frequently geographically displaced and also generally have small peer groups. It might be important, then, to engineer social learning opportunities for young people from different school communities to work together. This example illustrates one such opportunity.

The inclusion team from Oak Park Special School were reflecting on the conversations they had been having with a group of teenage girls about clothes and make-up. The girls had few opportunities out of school to meet up, go into town, and shop for their own clothes. The inclusion team coordinator instigated a meeting with a teacher from the local secondary school where they both agreed to pilot a programme called 'The Fashion and Beauty Group'.

A group of eight Year 10 girls from St Michael's High School who were taking a Health and Social Care course volunteered and joined with a group of five Key Stage 4 girls from Oak Park Special School for an opportunity for the latter to meet with other teenage girls. The Fashion and Beauty Group met once a fortnight for two terms at the high school facilitated by two people from the Oak Park inclusion team. Before their first meeting, the teachers met each group of girls separately. The girls from St Michael's participated in disability awareness training and a discussion about their perceptions of disability. They were introduced to the Oak Park girls through their personal profiles. These simple profiles served as individual introductions with name, age, what people like and admire about them, their interests and likes/dislikes. The teachers told them that two of the girls were wheelchair users. The girls from St Michael's then completed their own personal profiles and the teachers shared them with the Oak Park group.

The two groups of girls met, looked at fashion magazines, and tried out new hairstyles on one another and used make-up – some for the first time. They visited clothes shops in the city centre, helped one another choose clothes, and tried on different fashions. They took photos and later used these as prompts for discussions about what suited different people. They watched and talked to each other and said they looked forward to attending the group. All of the girls made a choice to attend the group on each occasion.

The pilot group finished at the end of the spring term. Three months later, the inclusion coordinator asked for volunteers from the high school to join a second group and she was overwhelmed by the number of girls requesting to join on recommendation from the previous group. The Oak Park girls have all requested to join again and asked if three more of their friends can join. One girl told them: 'I am choosing all my own clothes now. And look, you told me I always wear plain clothes, I'm wearing stripes.' Another of the girls is sitting much straighter in her wheelchair with her head up and is talking in sessions, whereas previously she rarely participated in this way. The students from both schools were seen to be interacting and collaborating in their learning and discovery. The teacher and learner roles shifted, as all were working in a new and different context, and the parameters of the group allowed for democratic, participative practice in the group planning of sessions.

Discussion

Here, we draw on the above examples to discuss the possibilities and challenges for a democratic classroom.

Hargreaves (2004, p. 7) defines pupil participation as:

> ... how students come to play a more active role in their education and schooling as a direct result of teachers becoming more attentive, in sustained or routine ways, to what students say about their experience of learning and of school life.

Examples 1 and 2 illustrate the development of participation processes at one specialist setting where staff were clearly *becoming more attentive* to the 'voices' of the students. For some children and young people, including Michael, *listening* to their 'voice' involves *looking* as well (Lancaster & Broadbent, 2003), observing, actively 'doing', and building a relationship together. Understanding and interpreting a pupil's communication in this way enables others (like his teacher, Emma), perhaps, to have some appreciation of the pupil's perspective and then to act as advocates, formally or informally (ibk initiatives, 2004), for the pupil. There are, of course, potential difficulties and challenges when advocacy is involved. How do we really know that the child's or young person's views are faithfully and accurately portrayed? How do we really know what Michael means? Why should we take Emma's perspective as being any closer to Michael's view than his support worker's perspective or that of his family, for example? Does the process of gathering information through this approach continue to privilege professionals/adults?

Gathering information about pupils frequently takes the form of teacher observation and teacher assessment, often against some form of 'objective' norms (for example, National Curriculum standards). The approach to gathering information with, about, and for Michael in Example 2 illustrates some possibilities for 'pedagogical documentation' that embody different, more democratic principles. As Moss (2007, pp. 14–15) states:

> It is important to keep in mind that pedagogical documentation is not child observation; it is not a means of getting a true picture of what children can do, nor a technology of normalisation. It does not, for example, assume an objective, external truth about the child that can be recorded and accurately represented. It adopts instead the values of subjectivity and multiplicity: it can never be neutral, being always perspectival.

Moss (2007) draws on the *Mosaic Approach*, a framework for listening (Clark & Moss, 2001, 2005) that can be applied with children and young people of all ages. This approach incorporates a range of methods, recognizing the different 'languages' or voices of children and young people. It is participatory, by treating children as experts and agents in their own lives, and reflexive, by including children, practitioners, and parents in reflecting on meanings and addressing the question of interpretation (Clark, 2010; Clark & Moss, 2005). Such pedagogical documentation would seem to offer possibilities for a more democratic classroom.

There is an interesting interplay in person-centredness – simultaneously, there is a focus on individuals and also a focus on community values (Dowling et al., 2007). Here we can also see Beane's two principles of democracy – individual human dignity and regard for others. On the one hand, person-centred approaches promote individual autonomy and independence; on the other hand, they imply a community base (for example, the community of girls in the Fashion and Beauty Group and Michael's friends and family helping to decide what is important for him). Robertson et al. (2005) evaluated person-centred planning in the health and social care systems and noted its effectiveness in improving the life experiences of adults with learning disabilities, but they also raise an ethical point: why do we need to develop these special ways of support so that people with learning disabilities are treated in the same way as anyone else in society? Here, we note the dilemma in recognizing difference (Norwich, 2007). If we treat pupils the same, we neglect any considerations of difference and this may not provide adequately for some children. However, if we treat some children differently (for example, providing person-centred plans for some children only), we may stigmatize and perhaps perpetuate inequalities. By its very nature, 'special education' has a history of separate practices, often regarded as 'technical' and requiring specialist knowledge (Thomas & Loxley, 2007) – for example, the use of tightly defined behavioural objectives and individual education plans. Such 'technical' practice is used to govern children's actions to elicit specific developmental and predetermined outcomes. We suggest that democratic practice is different. Indeed, Slee (2001) suggests that democratic schools might liberate us from such traditional notions and practices of special education. Person-centred planning done badly might look like a new version of individual education plans or individual learning plans or be reduced to a one-to-one tutorial to discuss what an individual wants to learn (Jacobsen, 2006), a technical and bureaucratic practice. This is why person-centred or democratic approaches must be more than a tool, more than procedure, more than an annual review process. In the Fashion and Beauty Group, difference seemed to be recognized, respected, and represented yet also reworked to ascertain sameness among the girls. Such processes need to be more than a pilot programme – they must be integral to the lived relations and experiences of children and young people and their teachers.

Concluding comments

If democracy is an idea about how people might live together, the democratic classroom is about how pupils, teachers, and other staff live and learn together. Educational initiatives, such as person-centred approaches, involve complex relationships between policy, people, and systems. As noted earlier, working in a person-centred and democratic way requires a cultural shift in the relationship between staff and children and young people. Democracy and participation are not things to be 'done to' or even 'done with' children and young people, but are part of an overall philosophy, a way of working. Participation and community are not just about adapting structures and systems and removing barriers, but about principled, ethical relationships. Within schools, staff at all levels must view all pupils as active participants, as choice-makers, as meaning-makers (Lawson, 2003). As Knight (2001) says, a democratic classroom cannot be delivered, it must emerge. It is not about asking people to do anything more, it is about asking people to do things differently.

Earlier, we noted the constraints of schooling and the autocratic nature of schools. We have taken aspects of a democratic approach and illustrated possibilities and challenges for a democratic classroom, emphasizing the role of the staff. However, within the constraints of the current education system, the potential for a democratic classroom seems remote. It might be possible, as we have illustrated, to develop elements of democratic practice within a classroom or school. This requires staff taking a principled and ethical approach, but they need to be honest, reflexive, and realistic with themselves and their students about the true extent of this participation.

Acknowledgements

The authors would like to thank to Emma Kenshole, Sam Gosling, and Ellen Tinkham School, Exeter.

8

MARTIN HANBURY
Relationships in and around the classroom

Introduction

At the heart of all good learning lies a positive and enduring relationship between the learner and the teacher. This chapter explores how positive relationships can be secured and maintained through an understanding of the complex and dynamic interplay between learner, teacher, and the context in which they co-exist.

Alongside this understanding, I examine how educationalists might develop ethically based pragmatic approaches to a range of challenging circumstances. There is no single simple solution to myriad complex situations educationalists encounter. But there are processes that enable us to uncover solutions that are pertinent to our context and lie somewhere hidden within us.

Throughout the chapter, there is an understanding that notions of *relationships* and *pupil behaviour* are inextricably woven together. At an obvious level, pupils' behaviour portrays the nature of their relationships with others. At a more subtle level, pupils' behaviour and the relationships they experience with others co-determine one another. At an obvious level, these notions are bound together; at a subtle level, they are intermingled.

The foundations of learning

Some of our earliest instincts and intuitions are oriented towards learning how to become social beings and learning how to form relationships. The vast majority of infants do this extremely well and within weeks have learnt how to affect the world around them, forming bonds with parents, siblings, and their family network. This predisposition for interaction creates a dynamic in which infants affect the behaviour of adults, who, in turn, influence the developing behaviour of the child in a reciprocal, cyclic process. By the time children enter the educational system, they are experienced and skilled relationship builders with the potential to form and develop positive, enduring relationships with the people they encounter. These relationships are at the heart of their learning journey and our obligation as educators is to engage in this positive dynamic, thereby nurturing and leading the learning of the pupil.

For the great majority of pupils in our schools, educators are well equipped to provide the optimum conditions for relationships to thrive. Educators are motivated by the intrinsic value of working with pupils, they enjoy the company of children and young people, and they understand the benefit to themselves of these rich and positive interactions. After all, educators are human too and have acquired and never lost the same drives for interaction that the young people around them patently display. Therefore most pupils, in most schools enjoy strong and positive relationships that act as the foundation for their learning. The strength of these relationships is portrayed in the 2008–2009 Annual Report of Her Majesty's Chief Inspector (Ofsted, 2009), which noted that in 80 per cent of secondary schools behaviour is either good or outstanding, with the figure even higher in primary and special schools.

There are groups of pupils, however, who find difficulty in establishing and maintaining relationships. This can be for several reasons, including learning difficulties and disability, severe social disadvantage, poor mental health, and poor physical health. Often, these factors are compounded, presenting educators with a labyrinthine complex of difficulties that require highly skilled and sensitive approaches. It is important to state that pupils who experience difficulties in these domains do not necessarily experience difficulties in forming relationships; there is no predetermined causal link. Nevertheless, educators need to be mindful that pupils who do experience problems in these identified areas may well have connected difficulties in building and maintaining positive relationships with adults and their peers.

Indicators of this can be found in a number of sources related to exclusions for pupils with special educational needs and disabilities (SEND). Wilkin and colleagues (Wilkin, Archer, Ridley, Fletcher-Campbell, & Kinder, 2005) reported that pupils with Statements of Special Educational Need were four times more likely to be excluded than other pupils, while the *Times Educational Supplement* reported that pupils with SEND were eight times more likely to be excluded than their peers (Ward, 2009). Equally, there is evidence that pupils with SEND are often marginalized by their peers, with MENCAP and the National Autistic Society revealing that up to 80 per cent of pupils with SEND reported that they had been the victims of bullying (MENCAP, 2007). However these statistics are construed, there is clear evidence that for some pupils, the development of positive and enduring relationships is problematic.

Recognizing the fundamental importance of relationships in the learning process compels educators to actively engage with this complex issue and create the conditions in which positive relationships can thrive. Three essential factors support this process:

- *Understanding* the factors that are inhibiting the development of positive relationships.
- *Implementing* effective approaches to enable positive relationships.
- *Embedding* the capacity to build relationships within individuals.

By ensuring that each of these factors is present and operating in an interwoven and compatible manner, it is possible to create a climate in which strong relationships develop and young people succeed.

Understanding

The seminal work of LaVigna and Donnellan (1986) provided practitioners in the field of learning disabilities with the underpinning premise that, 'Human behaviour never occurs in a vacuum' (p. 18). Critically, human behaviour is a function of the context in which it occurs and exists in a dynamic interplay with that context, both shaping and being shaped by the conditions that surround it. Consequently, in endeavouring to understand our interactions with pupils and the behaviour pupils present, we need to develop a holistic understanding of the pupil based on the many factors that influence their lives. Clearly, it is impossible, and arguably undesirable to know everything about every pupil with whom we come into contact. However, a level of understanding needs to be acquired before we can develop effective strategies to support positive behaviour and, as a simple rule of thumb, the more complex the situation, the greater the depth of understanding required.

Developing this understanding is an organic process and does not lend itself easily to linear representations. However, educators need a starting point because, in the words of Ivan Turgenev (1860) in the novel *First Love*, 'If we wait for the moment when everything, absolutely everything is ready, we shall never begin.' Or, as cartoon character Dick Dastardly frequently said in *Stop the Pigeon*, 'Muttley, DO something!'

Initially, exploring an understanding of the learning context provides a backcloth against which the specifics of a pupil's behaviour can be considered. A critical component of the learning context is the adult working with the pupil; it is also the one component educators can consistently influence. Consequently, educators need to understand their role in the dynamics of their relationship with the pupil through a process that is neither defensive nor self-deprecating but rather presents a balanced and neutral view of the educator's influence on the conditions. We might ask, 'what effect do my qualities have on this situation?' For example, aspects of our practice that are hugely beneficial to most pupils, in most settings, may contain negative elements in a specific situation. Alternatively, we could enquire, 'how do my professional experiences equip me to teach this pupil?' For example, in encountering unusual conditions, we might reasonably expect to have no practical knowledge of strategies that support the pupil.

Whatever questions we choose to ask in order to form a picture of our impact on the relationship and the context in which that relationship exists, it is vital that we are fair, dispassionate, and driving towards solutions. To achieve this difficult, anodyne neutrality, educators may adopt a simple schedule as follows:

1   Write down a series of up to five questions examining their role around classroom relationships.

2   Respond to these questions some days later, perhaps with a trusted colleague or friend who can offer a triangulated viewpoint.

3   Create an action plan that emerges from the responses, in particular noting those areas of professional development that have been identified.

4   Engage those individuals or agencies that can support the implementation of the action plan.

Concurrent with this task, the learning environment must be forensically evaluated, accounting for both the physical layout and the cultural orientation. Just as we should ask searching questions of ourselves, so we should investigate the impact of the buildings, fixtures, and furnishings that pupils encounter. Crucially, we must consider the size of the spaces the pupils experience, the acoustics of these spaces, the amount of natural light available in them, and the state of repair and decoration within them. We need accurately to determine how safe and healthy spaces are, how access and egress are controlled, and how pupils transfer to and within these spaces. We must never underestimate the profound influence the physical environment has on our relationships with others and the concomitant impact on learning.

Similarly, there is a cultural context to consider. The ethos that pervades organizations has a profound effect on every learner and for pupils with SEN this is no different. Organizations must make a conscious and manifest effort to ensure that the cultural message they transmit actively encourages positive relationships and supports those pupils who may experience difficulties in forming relationships. It is not enough to contain this within a mission statement; it must imbue every action taken and inform every decision that is made.

Alongside developing an understanding of the context for learning, it is vital that we develop our understanding of the pupils themselves. It is only by developing this knowledge and understanding that educators can begin to create the conditions through which positive relationships can be secured and maintained. Clearly, human beings are deeply enigmatic, contradictory and complicated, and understanding them remains the quest rather than the grail. But what cannot be attained is still worth attaining and therefore, as educators, we must commit to understanding the pupils we work with as best we can.

In the first instance, it is necessary to define the parameters of need a pupil experiences. Often this draws us towards identifying a condition or, put more prosaically, 'labelling'. As discussed in Chapter 2, the issue of the label a pupil carries is, in itself, an ethically complex domain. Whether that label is a sign, a signifier, a signpost, a significance or a signature is deeply contestable, as is the notion of labelling itself. Nonetheless, for the foreseeable future pupils will continue to carry a label and educators will endeavour to respond to the needs commonly associated with that label. Moreover, as thinking around disability and SEN expands, so too will the already bewildering, kaleidoscopic taxonomy within the field. From a pragmatic point of view, educators should learn what they can about the generalities of the condition from reputable and traceable sources.

In considering the condition or conditions a pupil experiences, it is important that the educator maps their awareness of the condition onto the individual pupil and avoids crude and unhelpful generalities. Not all pupils with autism are aloof; not all pupils with visual impairment have great auditory skills; not all pupils with Down's syndrome love music. What remains critical is uncovering the individual pupil within the context of the condition and understanding the effect of the condition on the particular learner's capacity for building positive relationships.

Insight into how an individual is affected by the condition they experience can be gained through a close observation of behaviour. By observing and carefully analysing behaviour, educators can simultaneously develop their understanding of the pupil and their understanding of the behaviour that pupil exhibits. A basic tool in supporting this individualized approach is the use of functional analysis, which is defined as: 'An assessment process for gathering information that can be used to build effective behavioural support plans' (Mace, Lalli, & Pinter-Lalli, 1991, p. 155).

Functional analysis is based on the simple premise that all behaviour serves a purpose. While that purpose, or function, might not be obvious to others and might not be consciously identified by the individual, it is a powerful determinant in the way a person behaves. Consequently, to address the fundamental forces behind a given behaviour, it is imperative to identify the function of that behaviour. There are a number of formalized instruments for collecting information about the function of a behaviour, including the Motivation Assessment Scale (Durand & Crimmins, 1992). Equally, there is value in educators devising their own bespoke materials to navigate an understanding of the compelling factors driving behaviour in a specific context. Whatever approach is adopted, educators need to develop a rational and objective understanding of the purposes behind an individual's behaviour.

Achieving this understanding can lead educators away from counterproductive notions around the pupil's behaviour, such as when educators seek to account for behaviour as a separable consequence of the pupil's condition rather than the manifestation of a complex series of interactions and circumstances. Statements such as 'well a lot of pupils with X do that' or 'I'm never sure when he's just playing up or when it's his X kicking in' act as obstacles to developing a holistic view of the pupil and therefore militate against effective intervention. Rather, educators should be seeking deep understandings of what is going on within the whole pupil, understandings that are complex and need time to coalesce.

Although educators suffer the tyranny of the 'urgent' on a daily basis as we are driven towards instant successes, easy wins, and ever-improving attainment, we must resist the temptation to rush blindly onwards. Invariably, deep and enduring understanding is slow to form and cannot be expedited; if we are really to effect positive change for complex pupils, we must dedicate the time required for this process to take place and persevere in the face of pressures to affect a rapid solution.

Implementing effective approaches

The holistic understanding we develop around pupils operates at a largely theoretical level. It is the means by which we begin to discover how to build relationships with pupils and the lodestar that guides the evolution of those relationships. The practical manifestations of this understanding are the approaches and strategies that we introduce into our work with pupils. Ultimately, it is this pragmatic avatar of our relationships that has the most profound and enduring impact on pupils' well-being; it is the part of us that they experience.

When considering which approaches and strategies are most likely to be most effective in supporting the development of positive relationships, educators are compelled to address a fundamental ethical issue – namely, whether their treatment of pupils with SEN should be any different than their treatment of pupils with no significant barriers to their learning. For example, should different standards of behaviour be required of pupils with learning difficulties and disabilities than are required of their peers without such difficulties? Should the standards of behaviour required of pupils with SEND differ according to the context in which they are located? Should educators commit more time and energy to developing their understanding of pupils with SEND than they dedicate to understanding their peers? Central to these questions is the construct of disability and SEND that educators adopt. At one level, a construct of disability that is founded on the basis of equality could be seen to require equal expectations of all pupils. At another level, however, equal treatment does not determine the same treatment; equality exists in a complicated and shifting tension that is highly sensitive to the context in which it is located, as words attributed to Thomas Jefferson attest: 'There is nothing more unequal than the equal treatment of unequal people.'

Perhaps this conundrum is best resolved by exploring what our purpose for learning is for all pupils, regardless of their unique characteristics, abilities or circumstances. In this framing, equality lies in a fully inclusive pedagogy that is accessible to all learners. The means and methods by which that goal is attained may vary according to the context, in which case educators will actively seek to engage specified approaches to achieve the universal objective. However, the underlying principle of 'learning for all' should underpin each learning activity and be manifest in every element of practice.

Although differences should be respected and catered for, it is important to avoid absurd reductionism in which educators adopt competing, conflicting, and counterproductive expectations for each pupil. By constructing a coherent rationale for all our actions, educators can construct viable and ethically coherent positions that accommodate a breadth of approaches while respecting the central values of the school community. This often difficult and contentious journey requires consensus from across the whole learning community in which ethics are generated through discourse (Habermas, 1990).

Having established an ethical framework in which strategies can be located, educators are in a position to evaluate the nuts and bolts of learning within their organizations. Central to this is an examination of the relevance, suitability, and sustainability of the curriculum offered to pupils with SEN. To effect this examination, educators need to project the curriculum onto the individual pupil in question and ask:

Relevance

- How meaningful is the content of the curriculum to this pupil?
- How engaged with the content of the curriculum is this pupil?
- How will the content of the curriculum benefit this pupil in ten years?

Suitability

- How accessible is this curriculum to this pupil?
- What is the impact on other learners in making this curriculum accessible?
- Does accessing this curriculum compromise any pupil's dignity?

Sustainability

- Can we offer this quality of learning to all our pupils with SEN?
- Can we offer this quality of learning consistently for the next five years?
- Can we offer this quality of learning if key people leave our organization?

If this examination of the curriculum results in a positive evaluation of provision, then educators are able to focus on enhancing and further developing the curriculum for learners with SEN. However, in those circumstances in which an honest appraisal of the curriculum for learners with SEN concludes that it is irrelevant, unsuitable, and unsustainable, fundamental change is necessary. This necessitates a thorough and sometimes difficult process in which educators must challenge often long-standing assumptions and culturally embedded wisdoms within their organizations. Such radical activity must be supported by evidence and driven home with a coherent and enduring strategy as educators evolve an 'inclusive pedagogical approach [that] focuses on everybody in the community of the classroom' (Florian & Black-Hawkins, 2011, p. 820).

Where the curriculum for learners with SEND is appropriate, it is likely that other aspects of the provision will be supportive and positive. Organizations that are effective in providing high-quality education for pupils with SEND are characterized by a skilled and knowledgeable workforce that consistently demonstrates an open-minded, inclusive ethos. Implementing effective approaches for learners with SEND depends entirely on the people who work within the organization, and the creation and development of a high-quality staff team is a prerequisite in securing positive learning outcomes for learners with SEND. Put very simply, if we are to develop positive relationships for learners with SEND, we must ensure that those responsible for their learning want to be there and want to be with them.

However, it is often the case that the funding associated with supporting pupils with SEND is allocated on a short-term basis, presenting educational organizations with the Sisyphean task of recruiting members of staff on a short-term and insecure basis. Until finance for SEND is based around longer term, strategic funding models, the recruitment and retention of high-quality practitioners will remain problematic.

Nonetheless, there are many examples of high-quality practice in the field of SEND secured by the creation of high-quality staff teams. Such teams are developed by adhering to basic principles of workforce development and situating them in the context of SEND. Four fundamental components are required, namely:

- Recruitment
- Induction
- Development
- Extension.

In recruiting members of staff, it is of paramount importance that organizations are transparent and ambitious. Effective members of staff are clear about their role and motivated by their aspirations for learners with SEND. They understand their purpose and are fully aware of the situation they are entering. On joining a school community, members of staff naturally endeavour to understand the values and practices of that community and in this respect the induction process is vital. Induction should not be indoctrination but rather a process in which new colleagues are invited to understand and endorse the values of the learning community.

The complexity of many learners in this field requires that members of staff receive regular high-quality learning and development opportunities. As our ambition for learners with SEND extends, so too will the need to support those people working alongside them with the knowledge and understanding that befits their role. Finally, effective organizations invariably provide the opportunity for members of staff to extend beyond the scope of standard professional development and into innovative, challenging arenas. It is only by extending orthodox practice that we can meet the needs of those learners whose learning profile is unorthodox.

Establishing a suitable curriculum based around an inclusive pedagogy and engaging an effective, innovative workforce provides schools with the capacity to fulfil their statutory requirements. A raft of current legislation (Disability Discrimination Acts; Special Educational Needs and Disability Act and, more recently, the Equality Act (HMSO, 1995, 2001, 2005, 2010)) and the SEN Code of Practice (DfES, 2001b) determine that 'reasonable adjustments' are made by organizations to accommodate pupils' needs. In the best examples of practice, these reasonable adjustments are manifest as a highly personalized, bespoke learning programme made possible by a rich and varied curriculum based on the notion of learning for all.

In some circumstances, organizations may need to engage with specialist interventions to lever open access to learning for pupils. These interventions may derive from the specific requirements of a pupil's condition, designed by practitioners within that domain over many years. Some interventions may require very little adaptation of the learning context, whereas others may require wholesale environmental changes. There may be tensions between the ease with which one element of a pupil's programme can be delivered and the challenges presented by a different aspect of the programme for the same pupil. Equally, tensions and dilemmas may emerge for schools when one pupil with SEND presents as more easily accommodated than another pupil with SEND.

The implementation of effective approaches that support the development of positive relationships in our learning communities is fraught with tensions, complications, and conflicts. This is an inevitable consequence of the complexity of the ethical, pedagogical, and pragmatic questions that emerge from the field. We cannot, and arguably should not, avoid the problematic nature of the field, but rather ensure that our structures and organizations are intelligently pliable and able to flex with the demands of the tensions they experience. If teaching is too inflexible, we can expect fractures and fissures – and it is the learners who fall through these.

Embedding the capacity

The best of practice endures and the strongest of relationships are enduring. As educators we have a moral obligation to equip the learners we work alongside with the capacity to build and maintain positive relationships outside the classroom and beyond their school life. We should not be content with enabling learners to behave appropriately in a restricted number of lessons or within a specific locale or a specific subject area. Our aim must be to enable learners to transfer their relationship skills to as wide a range of contexts as possible and embed these skills such that they are skills for life.

This endeavour may well result in learning in the area of building relationships to be slower than if there were a simplistic focus on the here and now. Clearly, enabling the development of the necessary skills for building relationships within a restricted domain is likely to be quicker than a more ambitious programme for learners. This is because, in the latter case, educators are focusing on developing learners' capacity to shape the relationships they form rather than becoming passive participants in a relationship. This requires the steady acquisition of skills, many of which are learned through experiences, some of which may be difficult.

In this approach, educators must be careful to attain a balance between moving a learner forward too quickly and therefore not allowing time for skills to embed, and causing the learning process to stall as the learner becomes overwhelmed by difficulties. Fundamentally, throughout this process the educator is seeking to empower the learner by providing a broad range of relationship-based experiences. This process of empowering students provides pupils with strengths and skills in the key areas of:

- Self-assurance
- Selectivity
- Initiation maintenance
- Non-dependence.

Self-assurance

Many pupils with SEND have a long history of conflict with orthodoxy and perceived failure. Consequently, many pupils with SEND are not assured or confident, although for some a well-constructed bravado may obscure this. Yet successful relationships are based on a shared concept of the equal value of each partner in that relationship. From this, trust and mutual respect emerge as the cornerstones on which the relationship is built. If an individual has a limited sense of self-worth due to their experiences of failure, it is likely that there will be a proportionate limit to the domains in which that person feels confident and assured. Consequently, there will be limitations to the context in which that person experiences successful relationships; put simply, they will only experience positive relationships in those contexts in which they feel good about themselves.

Therefore, if educators are looking to broaden the contexts in which individuals secure positive relationships, they need to broaden the contexts in which those individuals feel successful and valuable. This involves exposing both the individual and also the context to mutually positive experiences through a sensitive, responsive, and structured programme that promotes the learner's sense of self-worth and educates the context in the value of the individual. Over time, the individual comes to expect success rather than failure and therefore brings to relationships a sense of self-worth and a concomitant self-assurance, thereby levelling the dynamics of the relationship from the start.

Selectivity

Generally, pupils with SEND have little choice about whom they are asked to form relationships with. In many of the most progressive learning environments, pupils with SEND are 'given' a buddy, 'allocated' a key worker or 'provided' with resources to assist their learning. It is ungracious to disregard the importance of these benefits but it is important to reflect on the extent to which pupils with SEND are active partners in shaping their learning. Clearly, a relationship is far more likely to be positive if all parties have had some degree of choice in the formation of the relationship and have chosen to be together. This entitlement to choose partners in relationships also ensures that the level dynamic discussed above is observed and respected.

Initiation maintenance

If learning has been in some way disrupted, it may well be that the individual has not acquired the early, elementary skills of relationship formation. The tongue-tied adolescent we have all been provides some insight to this for all of us when, desperate though we are to connect with a person, we either spend an excruciating eternity saying nothing or unleash a load of gibberish onto the object of our desire. For a pupil with SEND, this terrible awkwardness can characterize every attempt to form a relationship; it is little wonder that the motivation to do so evaporates.

Educators can support learners through this awkward initiation phase by providing a range of strategies that enable individuals to rehearse interactions. Some interventions, such as the Social Use of Language Programme (Rinaldi, 1992) and Social Stories (Gray & White, 1992), are commercially available and have proved value, although educators might decide to create their own structured programmes based around the specific needs of the individual learner. Although interactions may at first be a little stilted, over time and with consistent practice learners become more relaxed and fluent in their interactions.

No positive human relationships are static; therefore, having successfully formed relationships, it is critical that the skills of maintaining the relationship are developed. This will involve enabling learners to recognize the way in which relationships change as partners grow in their understanding of one another. Clearly, this learning is essentially experiential and educators need to consider the ethics around exposing individuals to potentially difficult emotional experiences.

Non-dependence

If any party in a relationship becomes too dependent on another, then the dynamics of the relationship become distorted. Where an individual may have struggled for some time to form positive relationships, there may be some element of insecurity threaded through their interactions with others that leads to an acquired dependency. It is therefore important for educators to build into all programmes an insurance against the individual becoming too dependent on others. This in itself will slow the process of skills development, as it requires the learner to transfer attributes across a number of differing partners. However, the longer term benefits determine that this pace is appropriate and necessary.

By empowering individuals and embedding the knowledge and understanding they acquire, it is possible to enable learners with SEND to develop an enduring and portable set of skills that support the development of positive relationships beyond the confines of the classroom and into adult life. If our purpose as educators is to help learners develop holistically, we need to think of the learner beyond our experience of them and into a world they will inhabit that will remain unknown to us. This requires imagination and creativity and adds to the excitement and intrigue of working with learners with SEND.

Conclusion

Developing positive relationships with pupils provides the foundation for all good learning experiences. The quality of pupils' learning is directly related to the strength of the relationships they experience and it is therefore imperative that educators take the time and expend the energy necessary to form and maintain strong and enduring relationships with pupils. Pupils with SEND present the educator with a unique opportunity to develop a pedagogy that is firmly situated around the interactions between the learner and the context in which they learn. This group of pupils, all too often portrayed as somehow problematic, actually represent our best chance of creating a first-class twenty-first century educational system. If we can get it right for our most vulnerable learners, we can get right for all.

9

DAVID ARMSTRONG
The ideal school?

Introduction

I start this chapter with three thought-provoking quotations:

> The Green Paper is about the children and young people in this country who are disabled, or identified as having a Special Educational Need. It is about their aspirations or hopes. Their desire to become, like every child and young person, independent and successful in their chosen future, and, to the greatest extent possible, the author of their own life story.
> (DfE, 2011b, Foreword by Michael Gove and Sarah Teather)

> The great enemy of clear language is insincerity. When there is a gap between one's real and one's declared aims, one turns as it were instinctively to long words and exhausted idioms, like a cuttlefish spurting out ink. In our age there is no such thing as 'keeping out of politics'.
> (George Orwell, 1947, 'Politics and the English language')

> 'Bitzer,' said Thomas Gradgrind. 'Your definition of a horse.'
> 'Quadruped. Graminivorous. Forty teeth, namely twenty-four grinders, four eye-teeth, and twelve incisive. Sheds coat in the spring; in marshy countries, sheds hoofs, too. Hoofs hard, but requiring to be shod with iron. Age known by marks in mouth.'
> 'Now girl number twenty,' said Mr Gradgrind. 'You know what a horse is.'
> (Charles Dickens, 1854, *Hard Times*)

Consider the above quotes: they span over 150 years but disclose several fundamental truths or 'deep ideologies' (Robinson, 2010) about education in the UK and elsewhere. For example, in current UK schools 'girl number twenty', Sissy Jupe, might be described as 'at risk' of social, emotional and behavioural difficulties or another form of special educational needs and disability (SEND) – particularly given that she lags behind her classmates in academic achievement. Then, as now, she does not 'fit' in with a rigid regime based around facts and attainment. For Sissy what matters is happiness and security rather than conforming to a system that prizes utility, linearity, and conformity (Robinson, 2010). Sissy is, arguably, disconnected from a flawed education system and instead connected to a more coherent view of the world and her life within in it. In this sense, Sissy is like many children with (or without) SEND in the UK, who psychologically self-cope in spite of often hugely unfavourable circumstances at home and at school (Armstrong & Humphrey, 2009; Mowat, 2009).

Taken as a whole, this book suggests some of the many tensions and contradictions inherent in special educational needs (SEN) policy and educational practice in the UK (see Chapters 1 and 3). Such contradictions arise at least partly because of the philosophical and moral depth of the questions that this area raises about what education is or should be for all children (Pumfrey, 2010). Previous chapters have examined facets of educational practice in the face of a drive for recognizing the wider needs of a child with a disability or difficulty with learning (DfES, 2001b, 2004b). They have explored this wider notion of education in light of the possibilities it discloses, specifically: the role of counselling in current educational practice (see Chapter 5); the wider place of psychology in the classroom (see Chapter 6); the relevance of labelling children (see Chapter 2); the implications of increased participation by children in their education (see Chapter 7); the possible future role for inclusion in UK policy and practice (see Chapter 3); the wider resonances of society within the school itself (see Chapter 4); and an emphasis on relationships rather than 'behaviour' (see Chapter 8).

What follows summarizes key points of previous chapters but interweaves them, together with other accounts, into an imaginary 'ideal school' for the reader. This might be described, to some extent, as a thought experiment (see Gendler, Tamar, & Hawthorne, 2002; Schick & Vaughn, 2010) with the aim of allowing the reader to visualize, explore, and draw conclusions from visiting this imaginary place. In keeping with offering the reader space to think (see the Introduction to this book), the rest of this chapter is intended to provoke reflection on 'what is' by exploring what 'might be'. This has a particular import at this moment. At the time of writing, the future of SEN and of inclusion are, to say the least, highly unclear. Possibilities stretch out: some potentially disastrous for the lives and education of millions of vulnerable children; others are less damaging or ambiguous; some futures might, instead, lead to a positive and historic transformation in education, with the education of children currently described as having SEND acting as a catalyst for major change (see Norwich, 2010; see also Chapters 1 and 3). It is important to note that the following ideal school is also, in several ways, a case study: as such, it is subjective. For example, in what follows, the concept of some additional need is retained – albeit 'additional support' rather than SEN. It might be that you, the reader, decide that this is unnecessary and would see the abolition of any systematic notion of difference in terms of support required. In this respect, your thoughts and personal reflections are vitally important: scepticism is very healthy here and entirely in keeping with the philosophy of this book. To support this, two blank pages appear at the end of the chapter, which are intended for your reflections on this chapter and on the book as a whole.

The conclusion to this chapter revisits the above debates, reiterating their importance, and offers final thoughts. These discussions draw out some of the deeper political dimensions to our possible ideal school and which underpin this book.

An ideal school?

Gone are the rowed windows often set in a drab, or even shabby, exterior and which suggest a depressing conformity to children and staff alike (Edgerton, McKechnie, & McEwen, 2011). The school façade is varied in construction and has glass elevations that reveal its interior, allowing light to enter into the building's core. The school is resolutely modern in architectural style/form and surrounded by carefully considered and planted grounds. In recognition of the ethical values promoted by the school, the building itself has a high environmental rating in its construction and maintenance of internal environment. There are glimpses of gardens and greenhouses that are tended by students, who grow fruit and vegetables. At our ideal school, the notion of an outdoor curriculum is strong and students have a range of activities to choose from – the outdoor curriculum includes, but is not defined by, activities based around sport. These are spaces for children to develop in and challenge themselves physically (Rigolon & Alloway, 2011). The wider health value of learning outside the classroom is recognized in the ideal school and children with wider emotional needs often find refuge in these activities when faced with difficult home lives or personal issues. There are also strong links with an external outdoor education provider whose staff work with children to develop their skills in areas such as rock-climbing. The school provides regular residential weekends in conjunction with outdoor educators: children on free school meals have assured places. Alongside and linked into the modern form of this 11–19 school is a less imposing, but no less modern, single-storey structure: this is the primary school. Staff from both co-located schools work closely together – younger children regularly visit the 11–19 school and vice versa. Facilities, such as the working gardens, are shared. For younger children, this lessens the difficulty of transition at age 11 (Bulkeley & Fabian, 2006). For them the 'big school' is very familiar and exciting. Some of the older students, who are interested in childcare or teaching, have valuable taster work experience within the primary school.

We walk into the large open atrium that serves as the entrance and key communal area; there is light streaming through the glass ceiling and a hubbub of activity. Different types of learning space blend into each other in subtle ways. Many spaces are informal and flexible spaces in which students sit in small groups working on problems or projects. In the ideal school, there is an important emphasis on children internalizing and mastering 'thinking skills' and the forms of self-study that support these (Hewitt, 1998). Children with forms of what we would describe as SEND – but are described as additional support needs here (Pumfrey, 2010) – benefit greatly from explicit attention to how they learn. A sense of identity and belonging is promoted in various forms and permeates the school (Reasoner & Lane, 2007). One small example is the large colourful wall curving around behind reception that hosts a picture of every current student and also presents something that is important to them: this could be a piece of artwork they have produced, a poem, a line from a song, anything that has personal meaning. Student work and art produced by students are evident throughout this main school space and in smaller class spaces. It is recognized that all children deserve a stimulating and pleasant physical environment, and that the learning environment plays a more substantive role in the educational process of children with additional needs (Frederickson & Cline, 2009, p. 199).

As we continue into the building it becomes clear that, culturally, the ideal school is far more relaxed, informal, and less institutional than many currently in the UK. Teachers do not uniformly wear suits or other formal clothes and there are no bells telling children when a lesson has ended. This hints at the deeper differences between our world and this ideal.

When we speak to the head teacher, some of these differences are clearly articulated. For her what matters is the quality of interactions between staff and all children. Strong and positive relationships are central to the values of the ideal school for all children but an emphasis on positive relationships benefit those with additional needs in particular (see Chapter 8). A child's progress is assessed against their individual needs rather than in unhelpful scholastic comparison with their peers or against absurd national targets. This approach is essential for children with additional needs, where 'adequate' progress does not involve catching up with peers but rather resides in meeting the wider needs identified by the child and his or her family (see Chapter 1). Neuropsychological concepts, such as working memory, also have a strong presence in thinking about a child's progress and their needs because it is recognized that these are fundamental to learning in all areas (see Alloway, Gathercole, Kirkwood, & Elliot, 2009). The head teacher acts as a collegial figure involving colleagues in decision-making wherever possible or practicable. This is not only seen by the head teacher as ethical but also as far more effective for staff performance than any 'top-down', authoritarian management style, which as she is very aware, often stifles creativity and innovation among colleagues (Priestley, Miller, Barrett, & Wallace, 2010). Professional autonomy, with support where needed, is part of school culture: it is recognized that staff (like children) require this to develop a sense of mastery over their own skills and for a sense of personal effectiveness. Consequently, micro-managing the everyday work of teachers is seen as unethical, disempowering, and ultimately pointless.

Distortions created by what might be described as the 'Excel approach to education' in the real UK are not evident in this ideal school. The head teacher does not need to waste valuable time and energy manipulating or fictionalizing data to ensure maximum funding for children or ensuring the best public relations profile for a variety of governmental bodies. There are no divisive school performance measures or league tables (see Chapter 1). The head teacher, together with other senior staff, advocates a minimum approach to administration. She would see our current educational bureaucracy as: detracting from the actual learning of children; often containing fictional 'data' anyway; ethically unsound in obsessively measuring and categorizing children; and often best dealt with by an administrator for a more efficient division of labour and better end result.

After speaking to the head teacher, we realize that this school has what might be described as a strong bias in favour of inclusion (see Chapter 3). The emphasis is on meeting the needs of all those who attend whatever their need, through high-quality 'mainstream' provision and high-quality teaching, with realistic resources to match these aspirations. Many of these differences between our world and this ideal spring from a historic, long-term, cross-political commitment (or 'covenant') to radically renew and substantially invest in education in the UK. In our ideal world, this historic agreement followed coordinated bottom-up agitation by teachers, parents, young people, and educationalists who made it clear that children with SEND were being disfavoured by a contradicted, anachronistic, and disordered system, along with many of their peers without SEND (Robinson, 2010). In addition, they pointed out that the UK was in danger of not meeting international obligations in this area (see Chapters 1 and 3). In our ideal world, politicians and other influential individuals eventually accepted that education simply had to receive far greater long-term investment: to argue against this was simply not acceptable. Several prominent MPs lost their parliamentary seats due to concerted campaigns because they would not accept this point.

A realistically resourced approach is evident in our ideal school in terms of those essential professionals who support teachers in their work with children. The school educational psychologist is often seen around the school, is based here for 80 per cent of his working week, and has substantial weekly contact with staff and students.[1] Unlike the current UK, there has been no crisis in recruitment for the profession (British Psychological Society, 2010) and there is a real (as opposed to a rhetorical) recognition that educational psychologists make a key contribution to improving the life chances of vulnerable children. Working via 'collaborative consultation' means that the school educational psychologist collaborates with teachers, children, and parents to propose possible interventions rather than positioning themselves as an 'expert' who has all the answers (McNab, 2009). In the ideal school, the teachers supported by the educational psychologist adopt a positive educational practice (PEP) framework (Clark, 2010; Clark & Moss, 2001, 2005). This takes a whole-school approach to: the fostering of positive emotions; working in a democratic person-centred way with the strengths that children have (see Chapter 7) rather than emphasizing deficits as we do now (described in Chapter 1); and a consequent sense of mastery and agency in *the children's* learning (see Chapter 5). This operates at many levels in our ideal school but one tangible part of the PEP approach is the extent of cooperative learning evident to an observer in and around classrooms; this helps children to learn to work together – with positive outcomes (Benard, 2004).

A key part of the educational psychologist's everyday role is to help teachers and children come to know themselves and each another, at a deeper level. This has a multitude of benefits that affect a child's behaviours towards others and self, their understanding of academic concepts, and their motivation and ability to learn with peers (Noble & McGrath, 2008). It is recognized that most children, at some point or other, but particularly those with additional needs who are at risk of school failure or exclusion, need help to self-regulate their emotions or learning (Blair & Diamond, 2008). This support involves explicit age-appropriate guidance on how to understand, plan, monitor, and evaluate their learning (or feelings) in a structured way (Zimmerman, 2008). All of this is supported by a professional culture and national system that treats children as children and as individuals, rather than as mini-achievers or pupils. This also affects how, and whether, individual assessments are carried out with the school educational psychologist (see Chapter 2). In consultation with other staff, he/she carefully considers whether this process is in the child's best interests and how the assessments help teachers to teach the child more effectively. Together they also consider whether any resulting label will actually add something unique to understanding and catering for the child's needs. In other words, this reasoning is driven by ethical, psychologically informed, and pedagogical factors, rather by a need for funding or wider bureaucratic reasons (see Chapter 3).

The educational psychologist introduces us to his close colleague: the school learning support coordinator (we might know them as the special educational needs coordinator). She describes her core role as enabling and supporting teaching staff to include children with diverse needs, with a small extra role in analysing data gathered about this. Teaching staff do not ask her for 'solutions' to children they teach or call her in to rescue them; nor is she an auditor of all paperwork related to SEND (Kearns, 2005). Staff development and staff support are, instead, major parts of her everyday role and in keeping with her role as a positive agent for change and development, she is also present at meetings of the senior management team where she represents these values (Hallett & Hallett, 2010). This role means that teachers are confident in their flexible and adaptive approach to teaching all of the children in their class.

Some children receive additional support for part of their time in school. The school learning support coordinator and educational psychologist both have strong relationships with local providers of additional, more specialist services for children. These are not, however, 'special schools', which have almost disappeared from the UK (see Chapter 3). Because staff have a strong strategic role in the school, and dedicated time to develop this, they are enabled to build this important dimension to support for children and they can, for example, call on specialist counselling (see Chapter 5).

Education officers from the local authority have helped to develop and support this strategic dimension to services offered.

At our ideal school, there is no need for tokenistic student forums: being attentive to the voices of children, particularly those who might be marginalized, is engrained in staff. Taking time to stop, step back, and listen carefully to children is valued. Teaching sessions often ask for children's views, perceptions, and understanding on issues and topics. This is done in a structured way with all learners, allowing them to build up the critical decision-making and thinking skills that they will need in later life (see Chapter 4). Our ideal school views all pupils as active participants, as choice-makers, as meaning-makers in their own learning (see Chapter 4). Children who have forms of SEND that affect communication or understanding are perceived as simply needing more support to develop and articulate their voice (Clark, 2010; Clark & Moss, 2001, 2005). In our ideal school, there are also semi-open internal spaces 'owned' by students, such as a student-run café that hosts expressions of voice and identity (bands, poetry nights, live performances). Developing children and young people's autonomy and personal responsibility are encouraged at every level of the school: it is recognized that this is far better in the long run in terms of developing internal motivation to develop and grow (Ryan & Deci, 2000), as opposed to obsessive adult monitoring of behaviour and compliance. A small number of well-trained teaching assistants are present in this ideal school but not due to the 'behaviour' of individual students. Instead, they support small groups of children on specific elements of their learning and often for short periods of time (see Chapter 1).

As we tour the well-equipped music suite that overlooks the gardens, we find out that several staff whom we might otherwise have met are away on study leave at the local university. In our ideal school, staff development (called 'professional learning') is seen as highly important. All teaching staff in particular have an entitlement to career-long appropriate professional learning with many studying for a master's degree and some for a doctorate. It has been accepted by successive UK governments that postgraduate qualifications are a core requirement for teachers' role as professionals, but especially in enabling them to meet the diverse needs of children. In our ideal school, this require-ment is met. The covenant described earlier funds one full day per week study leave for all staff registered on a master's course that is education related: this entitlement is not at the discretion of the head teacher but instead funded independently.

In offering master's study, local universities work together in a consortium, rather than in a fragmented, competitive, and independent way, to develop collective provi-sion for a geographical area of the UK. Institutions share staff and physical resources rather than replicate provision and expertise: this emphasis on collaboration enriches the experience of students and knowledge base of the scholars who teach them. This same model is used in undergraduate teaching degrees: these thoroughly prepare teachers for the diverse classrooms ahead, with substantive input on child develop-ment and child and adolescent psychology (Nash & Norwich, 2010). We discover that both the school learning support coordinator and the educational psychologist work one day per week at a local university. This is a valued part of their professional learning over the long term and also an enriching connection for students. When we ask the educational psychologist about what makes for good-quality staff development, he suggests that it should be 'ongoing and developmental, regular and most important of all, make us think more deeply about what we do in our professional lives and our reasoning – drawing out the underpinning theories and assumptions for critical reflec-tion'. The most important thing, he adds, is that 'we have the space to reflect and grow intellectually, away from the everyday demands of the job'. 'It's about widening our mental horizons, like all education' he suggests. On reflection, this is far from an emphasis on the benefits of qualifications for one's career, improved pay or any other one-dimensional gains (Webster-Wright, 2009). The purpose of education here draws on the notion that learning enriches the self and is worthwhile on this basis alone. This belief is something shared by educators, students, and parents – a deeper cultural value is assigned to learning *per se*, and by UK society generally, than in our world.

As we leave the vibrant hubbub of our ideal school, we pass a small fleet of shiny electric buses waiting to shuttle children home. There are few cars visible in the hazy early afternoon sun. Looking back at the ideal school, we consider the last comment about 'wider horizons'; compared with the real world that we know only too well, we reflect that this contains the deepest insight about this ideal. Teachers are part of a society, and of a culture, with a wider, richer, more confident view of its future.

A conclusion and some political implications

I suggest, following Orwell earlier, that it is impossible for educators and for the wider profession to be anything other than publically political and moral about education. Failure to argue, in moral and political terms, for a different future involving *all* children is, I suggest, at best to lose hope in a better future at all – a form of shared learned helplessness (Abramson, Seligman, & Teasdale, 1978). At its worst, such an absence of critical public voice by educators will accelerate the short-term, opportunistic, and destructive trends that teachers themselves frequently identify and which impact most on vulnerable children. Teachers are the key agent in changing the education system: articulating a critical voice, with children and with parents, is essential for positive change. If educators simply accept 'what is' in their professional lives, then they – and the children they teach – will increasingly be the victims of ill-informed governmental initiatives or commercial forces (increasingly the same thing). Politicians have shown themselves to be adept at appropriating education for their own ends, appealing to 'progress', the 'logic of the market', 'the inevitable', and citing an evidence base.

In response to the increasing use of terms such as 'progress' and 'reason' by establishment figures as justification for self-serving policies, Hind (2007) eloquently outlines a possible response. He suggests that by disenchanting ourselves and working collectively as disinterested partisans for truth, 'we might become what our guardians fear most, a critical mass'. He adds that 'our daring to know will help make another world possible' (Hind, 2007, p. 161). This connects with this chapter, where 'another world' is presented and, to some extent, with Chapter 5, where a role for practitioner-research is proposed in evaluating holistic services, such as counselling offered by schools. The usefulness of research in affecting educational transformation should, however, be viewed with caution. As Humphrey and colleagues note in Chapter 5, research is often cherry-picked by government to rationalize absurd initiatives that meet the political objectives of the week: 'research' is prone to political manipulation. Thomas Gragrind would approve of the current fetish for 'evidence-based' interventions and the intellectually impoverished 'impact' on practice metaphor (Saunders, 2011). Recognizing this suggests that the education of children should not be determined by what is written on pieces of paper, but should be informed instead by what is right, what is just, and what is compassionate for them and their families.

The most realistic prospect for radical change is that of a bottom-up or 'grass-roots' campaign against the inequities of the current system around SEND and in favour of a long-term settlement (or covenant) for children with additional needs. Research into innovation in human culture and the emergence of adaptively successful new self-organizing systems in nature suggests that bottom-up change can be a highly efficient driver in the social and political arena (Johnson, 1994). In his study of the birth of new ideas, Johnson (2010) reminds us that 'market-based competition has no monopoly on innovation' (p. 239). I would go further and argue that the current market-competition ideology in UK education is a major barrier to transforming and modernizing our current system. The one-dimensional demands of the market, for example, prevent the type of open-minded collaboration and creative networks that generate new (or as Johnson call them 'adjacent') possibilities. Current market-led logic in the UK education system often stifles the creative interactions between individuals (teachers, parents, children, tutors, researchers) and between institutions (schools, colleges, universities) that are necessary to enact creative, systemic change in meeting the many and varied needs of children. We might conclude that, contrary to the Green Paper (DfE, 2011b), an increased role for the market is travelling further down the cul-de-sac that began with the 1988 Education Act: it will only deepen the flaws that Cooper (2008) detects in the current system and that often marginalize children who are different alongside many who are typical.

Part of any hypothetical 'new deal' for children with SEND should be acceptance, by our political representatives, that international obligations on the rights of vulnerable children are met in full (UNESCO, 1994a), not just written on glossy paper or mentioned in glib emails for public consumption. Questions about the future of the current educational system around SEND hint at the varied, disordered, and often dysfunctional nature of current provision. This disorder is replicated at different levels: in the quality of initial teacher training and subsequent support (Nash & Norwich, 2010; Wedell, 2008); at the scale of meeting objectives in policy (see Goodman & Burton, 2010; see also Chapter 1); and reflected in the often unsatisfactory experiences of children with SEND, their families, and their teachers (Mowat, 2009).

As Norwich (2010) reminds us, any meaningful change here cannot occur without a 'transformed general system' (p. 109) because current provision, policy, and practice around SEND is so intertwined with the values, structures, and assumptions inherent more generally in the UK education system. An implication of this is that in challenging the current system around SEND and in advocating the moral responsibility of society towards vulnerable children, we are therefore promoting a very different future UK education system for all children: we are being deeply inclusive. Rebellion against 'what is' SEND – a category regarded by many as problematic to inclusion – could, ironically, bequeath a deeply inclusive legacy. That the future is ours to influence at this point is a potential burden, but also a possible privilege.

Note

1. In this ideal school, the educational psychologist is employed directly by the school. Currently in the UK there are around 2000–2500 educational psychologists (Atkinson & Squires, 2011; Atkinson et al., 2011; Squires & Farrell, 2006). In January 2010, there were 3333 state-funded secondary schools and 16,971 state-funded primary schools (DfE, 2011a). To make this 'ideal' a reality would require massive funding and training of educational psychologists – we would need approximately ten times the number that currently exist.

Space for your own reflection on this book

References

Abramson, L. Y., Seligman, M. E., & Teasdale, J. D. (1978). Learned helplessness in humans: Critique and reformulation. *Journal of Abnormal Psychology*, *87*(1), 49–74.

Aggett, P., Boyd, E., & Fletcher, J. (2006). Developing a Tier 1 CAMHS Foundation Course: Report on a 4-year initiative. *Clinical Child Psychology and Psychiatry*, *11*(3), 319–333.

Ainscow, M., Booth, T., Dyson, A., Farrell, P., Frankham, J., Gallannaugh, F. et al. (2006). *Improving Schools, Developing Inclusion*. London: Routledge.

Ainscow, M., & Miles, S. (2008). Making education inclusive for all: Where next? *Prospects*, *38*, 15–34.

Albano, A. M., & Kendall, P. C. (2002). Cognitive behavioural therapy for children and adolescents with anxiety disorders: Clinical research advances. *International Review of Psychiatry*, *14*, 128–133.

Allan, J. (2008). *Rethinking Inclusive Education: The Philosophers of Difference in Practice*. Dordrecht, Netherlands: Springer.

Alloway, T. P., Gathercole, S., Kirkwood, H., & Elliot, J. (2009). The cognitive and behavioural characteristics of children with low working memory. *Child Development*, *80*(2), 606–621.

Apple, M. W., & Beane, J. A. (Eds.) (1995). *Democratic Schools*. Alexandria, VA: Association for Supervision and Curriculum Development.

Armstrong, D., & Humphrey, N. (2009). Re-acting to a diagnosis of dyslexia among students entering FE: Development of the resistance accommodation model. *British Journal of Special Education*, *36*(2), 95–102.

Atkinson, C., Bragg, J., Squires, G., Muscutt, J., & Wasilewski, D. (2011). Educational psychologists and therapeutic interventions – preliminary findings from a UK-wide survey. *DECP Debate*.

Atkinson, C., & Squires, G. (2011). *Educational psychologists and therapeutic intervention: Promoting positive mental health*. Paper presented at the 3rd European Network for Social and Emotional Competence in Children.

Audit Commission (2002). *Special Educational Needs: A Mainstream Issue*. Wetherby: Audit Commission Publications.

Audit Commission (2008). *SEN/AEN VfM Resource Pack for Schools*. Retrieved 17 December 2010 from: http://www.sen-aen.audit-commission.gov.uk/Default.aspx.

Balchin, R. (2007). *Commission on Special Needs in Education: The Second Report*. London: Conservative Party Central Office.

Ballard, K. (Ed.) (1999). *Inclusive Education: International Voices on Disability and Justice*. London: Falmer Press.

Bandura, A. (1977). *Social Learning Theory*. New York: General Learning Press.

Barnsley Metropolitan Borough Council (2005). *Remaking Learning: Leading Change for Success*. Barnsley: Barnsley MBC.

Barton, L., & Tomlinson, S. (1984). *Special Education and Social Interests*. London: Croom Helm.

Baskin, T., Slaten, C., Corsby, N., Pufahl, T., Schneller, C., & Ladell, M. (2010). Efficacy of counseling and psychotherapy in schools: A meta-analytic review of treatment outcome studies. *The Counseling Psychologist, 38*(7), 878–903.

Baumeister, R. F., Campbell, J. D., Krueger, J. I., & Vohs, K. D. (2003). Does high self-esteem cause better performance, interpersonal success, happiness, or healthier lifestyles? *Psychological Science in the Public Interest, 4*, 1–44.

Beane, J. A. (2005). *A Reason to Teach: Creating Classrooms of Dignity and Hope*. Portsmouth, NH: Heinemann.

Benard, B. (2004). *Resiliency: What We Have Learned*. San Francisco, CA: WestEd.

Bercow, J. (2008). *The Bercow Report: A Review of Services for Children and Young People (0–19) with Speech, Language and Communication Needs*. London: DCSF.

Berel, S., & Irving, L. M. (1998). Media and disturbed eating: An analysis of media influence and implications for prevention. *Journal of Primary Prevention, 18*, 415–430.

Berger, K. S. (2005). *The Developing Person* (6th edn.). New York: Worth.

Best, R. (2002). *Pastoral Care and Personal-social Education: A Review of UK Research Undertaken for the British Educational Research Association*. Retrieved from: http://www.bera.ac.uk/files/reviews/best-pastoralcarepse.pdf.

Bielinski, J., & Ysseldyke, J. E. (2000). *Interpreting Trends in the Performance of Special Education Students*. NCEO Technical Report #27. Minneapolis, MN: University of Minnesota, National Center on Educational Outcomes.

Biesta, G. (2007). Foundations of democratic education: Kant, Dewey and Arendt. In R. van der Veen, D. Wildemeersch, J. Youngblood, & V. Marsick (Eds.), *Democratic Practices as Learning Opportunities* (pp. 7–18). Rotterdam: Sense.

Bines, H. (1986). *Redefining Remedial Education*. Beckenham: Croom Helm.

Blair, C., & Diamond, A. (2008). Biological processes in prevention and intervention: The promotion of self-regulation as a means of preventing school failure. *Development and Psychopathology, 20*, 899–911.

Blatchford, P., Bassett, P., Brown, P., Koutsoubou, M., Martin, C., Russell, A. et al. (2009a). *Deployment and Impact of Support Staff in Schools: Results from Wave 2, Strand 2*. London: DCSF.

Blatchford, P., Bassett, P., Brown, P., Martin, C., Russell, A., & Webster, R. (2009b). *Deployment and Impact of Support Staff Project*. Research Report RB148. London: DCSF.

Booth, T., & Ainscow, M. (1998). *From Them to Us: An International Study of Inclusion in Education*. London: Routledge.

Booth, T., & Ainscow, M. (2002). *Index for Inclusion: Developing Learning and Participation in Schools*. Bristol: CSEI.

Branden, N. (1994). *The Six Pillars of Self-esteem*. New York: Bantam.

British Psychological Society (2010). Resolving the crisis in training educational psychologists in England. *Debate, 137*, 26–27.

Brown, C. (1954). *My Left Foot*. London: Mandarin Books.

Bugental, J. (1964). The third force in psychology. *Journal of Humanistic Psychology, 4*(1), 19–25.

Bulkeley, J., & Fabian, H. (2006). Wellbeing and belonging during early childhood transitions. *International Journal of Transitions in Childhood, 2*, 18–30.

Burden, R. (2008). Is dyslexia necessarily associated with negative feelings of self-worth? *Dyslexia, 14*, 188–196.

Burden, R., & Burdett, J. G. W. (2005). Factors associated with successful learning in pupils with dyslexia: A motivational analysis. *British Journal of Special Education, 32*(2), 100–104.

Burman, E. (2005). Childhood, neo-liberalism and the feminization of education. *Gender and Education, 17*(4), 251–267.

Burns, R. (1982). *Self-concept Development and Education.* London: Holt, Rinehart & Winston.

Cain, D. (2002). *Classics in the Person-centered Approach.* Ross-on-Wye: PCCS Books.

Cajkler, W., Sage, R., Tennant, G., Tiknaz, Y., Tucker, S., & Taylor, C. (2007). *Working with Adults: How Training and Professional Development Activities Impact on Teaching Assistants' Classroom Practice (1988–2006).* London: EPPI-Centre.

Cann, A. (2007). Developing the understanding of self in secondary aged children with autism spectrum disorder. *Good Autism Practice, 8*(1), 49–63.

Carlock, C. J. (Ed.) (1999). *Enhancing Self-esteem* (3rd edn.). London: Taylor & Francis.

Cassen, R., & Kingdon, G. (2007). *Tackling Low Educational Achievement.* York: Joseph Rowntree Foundation.

Central Advisory Council for Education (England) (1967). *Children and Their Primary Schools. Vol. 1: Report.* London: HMSO.

Centre for Studies on Inclusive Education (1989). *The Integration Charter.* Bristol: CSIE.

Chan, S., & Quinn, P. (2009). Secondary school students' preferences for school counselors to be of the same ethnic origin as themselves. *Counselling and Psychotherapy Research, 9*(3), 210–218.

Chapman, C., Ainscow, M., Miles, S., & West, M. (in press). *Leadership that Promotes the Achievement of Students with Special Educational Needs and Disabilities.* Manchester: University of Manchester, School of Education.

Chapman, C., & Gunter, H. (Eds.) (2009). *Radical Reforms: Perspectives on an Era of Educational Change.* London: Routledge.

Clair, E., Church, R., & Bateshaw, M. (2002). Special education services. In M. Bateshaw (Ed.), *Children with Disabilities* (5th edn., pp. 589–606). Baltimore, MD: Brookes.

Clark, A. (2010). *Transforming Children's Spaces: Children's and Adults' Perceptions in Designing Learning Environments.* Abingdon: Routledge.

Clark, A., & Moss, P. (2001). *Listening to Children: The Mosaic Approach.* London: National Children's Bureau.

Clark, A., & Moss, P. (2005). *Spaces to Play: More Listening to Young Children Using the Mosaic Approach.* London: National Children's Bureau.

Cooley, C. H. (1902). *Human Nature and the Social Order.* New York: Scribner.

Cooper, M. (2006a). *Counselling in Schools Project, Glasgow, Phase II: Evaluation Report.* Glasgow: University of Strathclyde.

Cooper, M. (2006b). Scottish secondary school students' preferences for location, format of counselling and sex of counsellor. *School Psychology International, 27*(5), 627–638.

Cooper, M. (2009). Counselling in UK secondary schools: A comprehensive review of audit and evaluation data. *Counselling and Psychotherapy Research, 9*(3), 137–150.

Cooper, M., & McLeod, J. (2007). A pluralistic framework for counselling and psychotherapy: Implications for research. *Counselling and Psychotherapy Research, 7*(3), 135–143.

Cooper, M., & McLeod, J. (2011). *Pluralistic Counselling and Psychotherapy.* London: Sage.

Cooper, M., Rowland, N., McArthur, K., Pattison, S., Cromarty, K., & Richards, K. (2010). Randomised controlled trial of school-based humanistic counselling for emotional distress in young people: Feasibility study and preliminary indications of efficacy. *Child and Adolescent Psychiatry and Mental Health, 4*(12), 1–12.

Cooper, P. (2008). Like alligators bobbing for poodles? A critical discussion of education, ADHD and the bio-psychosocial perspective. *Journal of Philosophy of Education, 42*(3/4), 457–474.

Corrigan, P. W. (2006). Mental health stigma as social attribution: Implications for research method and attitude change. *Clinical Psychology: Science and Practice, 7*(1), 48–67.

Craig, C. (2007). *The Potential Dangers of a Systematic, Explicit Approach to Teaching Social and Emotional Skills (SEAL)*. Glasgow: Centre for Confidence and Wellbeing.

Creamer, E. G. (2000). Quality, equality, and equity in individual performance measures. In S. M. Janosik, D. G. Creamer, & M. D. Alexander (Eds.), *International Perspectives on Quality in Higher Education* (pp. 54–62). Blacksburg, VA: Educational Policy Institute of Higher Education.

Crocker, J., & Wolfe, C. T. (2001). Contingencies of self-worth. *Psychological Review, 108*, 593–623.

Cummings, C., Dyson, A., Jones, L., Laing, K., Scott, K., & Todd, L. (2010). *Evaluation of Extended Services. Thematic Review: Reaching Disadvantaged Groups and Individuals*. London: DCSF.

Cummings, C., Dyson, A., Jones, L., Laing, K., & Todd, L. (2011a). *Extended Services Evaluation. Thematic Review: The Role of Local Authorities*. London: DfE.

Cummings, C., Dyson, A., Muijs, D., Papps, I., Pearson, D., Raffo, C. et al. (2007). *Evaluation of the Full Service Extended Schools Initiative: Final Report*. Research Report RR852. London: DfES.

Cummings, C., Dyson, A., & Todd, L. (2011b). *Beyond the School Gates: Can Full Service and Extended Schools Overcome Disadvantage?* London: Routledge.

DCSF (Department for Children, Schools and Families) (2005). *Social and Emotional Aspects of Learning (SEAL): Guidance*. Nottingham: DCSF.

DCSF (Department for Children, Schools and Families) (2007). *The Children's Plan: Building Brighter Futures*. Cm 7280. London: DCSF.

DCSF (Department for Children, Schools and Families) (2008a). *21st Century Schools: A World Class Education for Every Child*. London: DCSF.

DCSF (Department for Children, Schools and Families) (2008b). *Children's Trusts: Statutory Guidance on Inter-agency Cooperation to Improve Well-being of Children, Young People and Their Families*. London: DCSF.

DCSF (Department for Children, Schools and Families) (2008c). *The Education of Children and Young People with Behavioural, Emotional and Social Difficulties as a Special Educational Need*. London: DCSF.

DCSF (Department for Children, Schools and Families) (2008d). *Targeted Mental Health in Schools Project. Using the Evidence to Inform Your Approach: A Practical Guide for Headteachers and Commissioners*. Nottingham: DCSF.

DCSF (Department for Children, Schools and Families) (2008e). *Working Together: Listening to the Voices of Children and Young People*. Retrieved from: www.teachernet.gov.uk/wholeschool/behaviour/participationguidance/.

DCSF (Department for Children, Schools and Families) (2009). *School Workforce in England (Including Local Authority Level Figures) January 2009 (Revised)*. London: DCSF.

DCSF (Department for Children, Schools and Families) (2010). *Guidance on Commissioning Targeted Mental Health and Emotional Wellbeing in Schools*. Nottingham: DCSF.

DCSF (Department for Children, Schools and Families) (undated). *Extended Services*. Retrieved from: http://www.teachernet.gov.uk/wholeschool/extendedschools/.

DCSF/DH (Department for Children, Schools and Families/Department of Health) (2007). *A Transition Guide for All Services: Key Information for Professionals about the Transition Process for Disabled Young People*. London: DCSF/DH.

DCSF/DH (Department for Children, Schools and Families/Department of Health) (2008). *Improving the Mental Health and Psychological Well-being of Children and Young People. National CAMHS Review: Interim Report*. London: DCSF/DH.

DCSF/DH (Department for Children, Schools and Families/Department of Health) (2009). *Healthy Lives, Brighter Futures: The Strategy for Children's and Young People's Health.* London: Central Office of Information for DCSF/DH.

DCSF/IDeA/LGA (Department for Children, Schools and Families/Improvement and Development Agency for Local Government/Local Government Association) (2007). *Narrowing the Gap in Outcomes.* Retrieved from: http://www.lga.gov.uk/lga/aio/21949.

DCSF/Ofsted (Department for Children, Schools and Families/Office for Standards in Education) (2009). *A School Report Card: Prospectus.* London: DCSF.

Delgado, S. V. (2008). Psychodynamic therapy for children and adolescents: An old friend revisited. *Psychiatry (Edgmont)*, 5(5), 67–72.

DES (Department for Education and Science) (1978). *Special Educational Needs: Report of the Committee of Inquiry into the Education of Handicapped Children and Young People (The Warnock Report).* London: DES.

Devon Children's Trust Partnership (undated). *Person-centred Approach.* Retrieved from: http://www.devonchildrenstrust.org.uk/pca/index.html.

Dewey, J. (1966). *Democracy and Education: An Introduction to the Philosophy of Education.* New York: Free Press.

DfE (Department for Education) (2010a). *Achievement for All.* Retrieved 5 May 2011 from: http://nationalstrategies.standards.dcsf.gov.uk/node/225595.

DfE (Department for Education) (2010b). *Children with Special Educational Needs 2010: An Analysis.* London: DfE.

DfE (Department for Education) (2010c). *Inclusion Development Programme.* Retrieved 5 May 2011 from: http://nationalstrategies.standards.dcsf.gov.uk/node/116691.

DfE (Department for Education) (2010d). *National Curriculum Assessments at Key Stage 2 in England, 2010 (Revised).* London: DfE.

DfE (2010e). *The Importance of Teaching: The Schools White Paper.* London: DfE.

DfE (Department for Education) (2011a). *DfE: Schools, Pupils and their Characteristics: January 2010.* Retrieved from: http://www.education.gov.uk/rsgateway/DB/SFR/s000925/index.shtml.

DfE (Department for Education) (2011b). *Support and Aspiration: A New Approach to Special Educational Needs and Disability – A Consultation (The Green Paper).* London: DfE.

DfEE (Department for Education and Employment) (1997). *Excellence for All Children: Meeting Special Educational Needs.* London: DfEE.

DfEE (Department for Education and Employment) (1998). *The National Literacy Strategy: Framework for Teaching.* London: DfEE.

DfEE (Department for Education and Employment) (1999). *National Healthy School Standard: Guidance.* Nottingham: DfEE.

DfES (Department for Education and Skills) (2001a). *Inclusive Schooling: Children with Special Educational Needs.* London: DfES.

DfES (Department for Education and Skills) (2001b). *Special Educational Needs Code of Practice.* Nottingham: DfES.

DfES (Department for Education and Skills) (2001c). *Special Educational Needs Code of Practice Toolkit.* Nottingham: DfES.

DfES (Department for Education and Skills) (2002). *Pupils, Teachers, Education Support Staff, Pupil:Teacher and Pupil:Adult Ratios in Maintained Schools in England: January 2002.* London: DfES.

DfES (Department for Education and Skills) (2004a). *Every Child Matters: Change for Children.* Nottingham: DfES.

DfES (Department for Education and Skills) (2004b). *Removing Barriers to Achievement.* London: DfES.

DfES (Department for Education and Skills) (2005a). *Excellence and Enjoyment: Social and Emotional Aspects of Learning (Guidance)*. Nottingham: DfES.

DfES (Department for Education and Skills) (2005b). *Extended Schools: Access to Opportunities and Services for All: A Prospectus*. London: DfES.

DfES (Department for Education and Skills) (2006a). *Excellence and Enjoyment: Social and Emotional Aspects of Learning: Key Stage 2 Small Group Activities*. Nottingham: DfES.

DfES (Department for Education and Skills) (2006b). *Primary Framework for Literacy and Mathematics*. Nottingham: DfES.

DfES (Department for Education and Skills) (2006c). *Publication of 2006 Test and Examination Results in the School and College*. London: DfES.

DfES (Department for Education and Skills) (2007). *Social and Emotional Aspects of Learning . . . Improving Behaviour . . . Improving Learning*. Retrieved 1 September 2007 from: http://www.standards.dfes.gov.uk/primary/publications/banda/seal/.

DH (Department of Health) (2001). *Valuing People: A New Strategy for Learning Disability in the 21st Century*. London: The Stationery Office.

DH (Department of Health) (2009). *Valuing People Now: A New Three-year Strategy for Learning Disabilities*. London: DH.

DH (Department of Health) (2010). *Person-centred Planning: Advice for Using Person-centred Thinking, Planning and Reviews in Schools and Transition*. London: DH.

Dickens, C. (1854). *Hard Times*. London: Penguin Classic.

Dowling, S., Manthorpe, J., & Cowley, S. (2007). Working on person-centred planning: From amber to green light? *Journal of Intellectual Disabilities, 11*(1), 65–82.

Downey, J. (2003). Psychological counselling of children and young people. In R. Woolfe, S. Strawbridge, B. Douglas, & W. Dryden (Eds.), *Handbook of Counselling Psychology* (3rd edn., pp. 322–342). London: Sage.

Driessen, G. (2007). The feminization of primary education: Effects of teachers' sex on pupil achievement, attitudes and behaviour. *International Review of Education, 53*(2), 183–203.

Duckworth, K. (2008). *The Influence of Context on Attainment in Primary School: Interactions between Children, Family and School Contexts*. London: Institute of Education, Centre for Research on the Wider Benefits of Learning.

Durand, V. M., & Crimmins, D. B. (1992). *The Motivation Assessment Scale*. Topeka, KS: Monaco & Associates.

Dyson, A., Farrell, P., Kerr, K., & Mearns, N. (2009). 'Swing, swing together': Multi-agency work in the new children's services. In C. Chapman & H. Gunter (Eds.), *Radical Reforms: Perspectives on an Era of Educational Change* (pp. 141–154). London: Routledge.

Dyson, A., Farrell, P., Polat, F., Hutcheson, G., & Gallanaugh, F. (2004). *Inclusion and Pupil Achievement*. London: DfES.

Dyson, A., & Gains, C. (Eds.) (1993). *Rethinking Special Needs in Mainstream Schools: Towards the Year 2000*. London: David Fulton.

Dyson, A., & Gallannaugh, F. (2007). National policy and the development of inclusive school practices: A case study. *Cambridge Journal of Education, 37*(4), 473–488.

Dyson, A., & Gallannaugh, F. (2008). Disproportionality in special needs education in England. *Journal of Special Education, 42*(1), 36–46.

Dyson, A., Gunter, H., Hall, D., Raffo, C., Jones, L., & Kalambouka, A. (2010). What is to be done? Implications for policy makers. In C. Raffo, A. Dyson, H. Gunter, D. Hall, L. Jones, & A. Kalambouka (Eds.), *Education and Poverty in Affluent Countries* (pp. 195–215). London: Routledge.

Dyson, A., Kerr, K., & Weiner, S. (2011). *Schools and Their Communities: Vision and Impact*. London: SSAT.

Dyson, A., & Millward, A. (2000). *Schools and Special Needs: Issues of Innovation and Inclusion.* London: Paul Chapman.

Ecclestone, K., & Hayes, D. (2008). *The Dangerous Rise of Therapeutic Education.* London: Routledge.

Edgerton, E., McKechnie, J., & McEwen, S. (2011). Students' perceptions of their school environment and their relationship with educational outcomes. *Educational and Child Psychology, 28*(1), 33–45.

Edwards, A., Lunt, I., & Stamou, E. (2010). Inter-professional work and expertise: New roles at the boundaries of schools. *British Educational Research Journal, 36*(1), 27–45.

Edwards, J. (1984). *The Scars of Dyslexia.* London: Continuum.

Equality and Human Rights Commission (2010). *How Fair is Britain? Equality, Human Rights and Good Relations in 2010. The First Triennial Review.* London: Equality and Human Rights Commission.

Estyn (2008). *Closing the Gap between Boys' and Girls' Attainment.* Cardiff: Estyn.

European Democratic Education Community (2011). *What is Democratic Education?* Retrieved from: http://www.eudec.org/democratic-education/.

Falvey, M. A., Givner, C. C., & Kimm, C. (2005). What is an inclusive school? In R. Villa & J. S. Thousand (Eds.), *Creating an Inclusive School* (3rd edn., pp. 1–12). Alexandria, VA: Association for Supervision and Curriculum.

Farrell, P. (2000). The impact of research on developments in inclusive education. *International Journal of Inclusive Education, 4*(2), 153–162.

Farrell, P., Alborz, A., Howes, A., & Pearson, D. (2010). The impact of teaching assistants on improving pupils' academic achievement in mainstream schools: A review of the literature. *Educational Review, 62*(4), 435–448.

Farrell, P., Dyson, A., Polat, F., Hutcheson, G., & Gallannaugh, F. (2007). The relationship between inclusion and academic achievement in English mainstream schools. *School Effectiveness and School Improvement, 18*(3), 335–352.

Fielding, M. (2004). Transformative approaches to student voice: Theoretical underpinnings, recalcitrant realities. *British Educational Research Journal, 30*(2), 295–311.

Florian, L., & Black-Hawkins, K. (2011). Exploring inclusive pedagogy. *British Educational Research Journal, 37*(5), 813–828.

Forlin, C., & Lian, J. (Eds.) (2008). *Reform, Inclusion and Teacher Education: Towards a New Era of Special Education in the Asia-Pacific Region.* Abingdon: Routledge.

Frederickson, N., & Cline, C. (2009). *Special Educational Needs, Inclusion and Diversity* (2nd edn.). Maidenhead: Open University Press.

Galletley, I. (1976). How to do away with yourself. *Remedial Education, 11*(3), 149–152.

Gee, K. (2004). Developing curriculum and instruction. In F. Orelove, D. Sobsey, & R. Silberman (Eds.), *Educating Children with Multiple Disabilities: A Collaborative Approach* (4th edn., pp. 67–114). Baltimore, MD: Brookes.

Geldard, K., & Geldard, D. (2009). *Relationship Counselling for Children, Young People and Families.* London: Sage.

Gendler, R., Tamar, S., & Hawthorne, J. (Eds.) (2002). *Conceivability and Possibility.* Oxford: Clarendon/Oxford University Press.

Gerber, P. J., Reiff, H. B., & Ginsberg, R. (1996). Reframing the learning disabilities experience. *Journal of Learning Disabilities, 29*, 98–112.

Giangreco, M. F. (2006). Foundational concepts and practices for educating students with severe disabilities. In M. E. Snell & F. Brown (Eds.), *Instruction of Students with Severe Disabilities* (6th edn., pp. 1–27). Upper Saddle River, NJ: Pearson Education/Prentice-Hall.

Gillon, E. (2007). *Person Centred Counselling Psychology*. London: Sage.

Goffman, E. (1963). *Stigma: Notes on the Management of Spoiled Identity*. New York: Prentice-Hall.

Goleman, D. (1995). *Emotional Intelligence*. New York: Bantam Books.

Goodman, A., Sibieta, L., & Washbrook, E. (2009). *Inequalities in Educational Outcomes among Children Aged 3 to 16: Final Report for the National Equality Panel, September 2009*. London: National Equality Panel, Government Equalities Office.

Goodman, R. L., & Burton, D. M. (2010). The inclusion of students with BESD in mainstream schools: Teachers' experiences of and recommendations for creating a successful inclusive environment. *Emotional and Behavioural Difficulties, 15*(3), 223–237.

Gray, C., & White, A. L. (1992). *My Social Stories Book*. London: Jessica Kingsley.

Greenberg, M. T., Siegel, J. M., & Leitch, C. J. (1983). The nature and importance of attachment relationships to parents and peers during adolescence. *Journal of Youth and Adolescence, 12*, 373–386.

Habermas, J. (1990). *Moral Consciousness and Communicative Action*. Cambridge: Polity Press.

Hall, J. (1996). Integration, inclusion: What does it all mean? In J. Coupe O'Kane & J. Goldbart (Eds.), *Whose Choice? Contentious Issues for those Working with People with Learning Difficulties*. London: Fulton.

Hallahan, D. P., & Kaufmann, J. M. (1994). *Exceptional Children: An Introduction to Special Educational Needs*. Englewood Cliffs, NJ: Prentice-Hall.

Hallett, F., & Hallett, G. (2010). *Transforming the Role of the SENCO*. Maidenhead: Open University Press.

Hanley, T., Sefi, A., & Lennie, C. (2011). Practice based evidence in school based counselling. *Counselling and Psychotherapy Research, ifirst* (DOI: 10.1080/14733145.2010.533778).

Hargreaves, D. (2004). *Personalised Learning: Student Voice and Assessment for Learning*. Retrieved from: http://www.ssat-inet.net/resources/publications/publicationdescriptions/personalisinglearningseries1.aspx.

Harlem Children's Zone (2009). *The HCZ Project: 100 Blocks, One Bright Future*. Retrieved from: http://www.hcz.org/about-us/the-hcz-project.

Harris, J. R. (1999). *The Nurture Assumption: Why Children Turn Out the Way They Do*. London: Bloomsbury.

Harrison, A. (2003). Change in psychoanalysis: Getting from A to B. *Journal of the American Psychoanalytic Association, 51*(1), 221–256.

Harrower, J. K. (1999). Educational inclusion of children with severe disabilities. *Journal of Positive Behaviour Interventions, 1*, 215–230.

Hart, R. A. (1992). *Children's Participation, from Tokenism to Citizenship*. Florence: UNICEF.

Harter, S. (1999). *The Construction of Self*. New York: Guilford Press.

Health Advisory Service (1995). *Together We Stand: The Commissioning, Role and Management of Child and Adolescent Mental Health Services*. London: The Stationery Office.

Hegarty, S. (1991). Towards an agenda for research in special education. *European Journal of Special Needs Education, 6*, 87–99.

Hewitt, J. P. (1998). *The Myth of Self-esteem*. New York: St. Martin's Press.

Hind, D. (2007). *The Threat to Reason*. London: Verso.

HM Government (2006). *Government Response to the Education and Skills Committee Report on Special Educational Needs (October 2006)*. London: The Stationery Office.

HMSO (His Majesty's Stationery Office) (1944). *Education Act 1944*. London: HMSO.

HMSO (Her Majesty's Stationery Office) (1981). *1981 Education Act: Chapter 60*. London: HMSO.

HMSO (Her Majesty's Stationery Office) (1995). *Disability Discrimination Act 1995*. London: HMSO.

HMSO (Her Majesty's Stationery Office) (2001). *Special Educational Needs and Disability Act 2001*. London: HMSO.

HMSO (Her Majesty's Stationery Office) (2005). *Disability Discrimination Act 2005*. London: HMSO.

HMSO (Her Majesty's Stationery Office) (2010). *Equality Act 2010*. London: HMSO.

Hoge, D. R., Smit, E. K., & Hanson, S. L. (1990). School experiences predicting changes in self-esteem of sixth- and seventh-grade students. *Journal of Educational Psychology, 82*, 117–127.

House of Commons Education and Skills Committee (2006). *Special Educational Needs: Third Report of Session 2005–06: Vol. 1*. London: House of Commons.

House of Commons Education and Skills Committee (2007). *Special Educational Needs: Assessment and Funding*. London: The Stationery Office.

Howe, M. J. A. (1997). *IQ in Question: The Truth about Intelligence*. London: Sage.

Howes, A. J., Davies, S. M. B., & Fox, S. (2009). *Improving the Context for Inclusion: Personalising Teacher Development through Collaborative Action Research*. London: Routledge.

Humphrey, H. (2003). Facilitating a positive sense of self in pupils with dyslexia: The role of teachers and peers. *Support for Learning, 18*, 130–136.

Humphrey, N. (2002). Teacher and pupil ratings of self-esteem in developmental dyslexia. *British Journal of Special Education, 29*(1), 29–36.

Humphrey, N. (forthcoming). The emperor has no clothes: Challenging the orthodoxy of the social and emotional aspects of learning programme.

Humphrey, N., Bartolo, P., Ale, P., Calleja, C., Hofass, T., Janikova, V. et al. (2006). Understanding and responding to diversity in the primary classroom: An international study. *European Journal of Teacher Education, 29*, 305–318.

Humphrey, N., Charlton, J. P., & Newton, I. (2004). The developmental roots of disaffection? *Educational Psychology, 24*, 579–594.

Humphrey, N., Lendrum, A., & Wigelsworth, M. (2010). *Secondary Social and Emotional Aspects of Learning (SEAL): National Evaluation*. Nottingham: DfE.

Humphrey, N., & Mullins, P. (2002a). Personal constructs and attributions for academic success and failure in dyslexia. *British Journal of Special Education, 29*, 194–201.

Humphrey, N., & Mullins, P. (2002b). Self-concept and self-esteem in developmental dyslexia. *Journal of Research in Special Educational Needs 2*.

Humphrey, N., & Squires, G. (2010). *Achievement for All Evaluation: Interim Report (May 2010)*. DfE RR 028. London: DfE.

Humphrey, N., & Squires, G. (2011). *Achievement for All: National Evaluation*. DfE RR 123. London: DfE.

ibk initiatives (2004). *An Advocacy Service for Disabled Children in Sheffield*. Sheffield: ibk initiatives.

Ireland, E., Kerr, D., Lopes, J., Nelson, J., & Cleaver, E. (2006). *Active Citizenship and Young People: Opportunities, Experiences and Challenges in and Beyond School (Citizenship Education Longitudinal Study: Fourth Annual Report)*. DfES Research Report 732. London: DfES.

Ireson, J., & Hallum, S. (2001). *Ability Grouping in Education*. London: Sage.

Jacobsen, Y. (2006). *Consultative Paper: Person-centred Planning and People with Learning Difficulties. What has it got to do with Post-16 Education?* NIACE/Valuing People Support Team. Retrieved from: http://sflip.excellencegateway.org.uk/PDF/E1–17_NIACE%20Consultative%20paper.pdf.

James, W. (1890). *Principles of Psychology*. New York: Dover.

Jenkins, P., & Polat, F. (2005). *The Current Provision of Counselling Services in Secondary Schools in England and Wales*. Manchester: University of Manchester.

Johnson, D. W., & Johnson, R. T. (1996). Cooperative learning and traditional American values: An appreciation. *NASSP Bulletin, 80,* 63–65.

Johnson, S. (1994). *Emergence: The Connected Lives of Ants, Brains, Cities and Software.* London: Penguin.

Johnson, S. (2010). *Where do Good Ideas Come From?* London: Wheatsheaf.

Jupp, K. (1992). *Everyone Belongs.* London: Souvenir Press.

Kamins, M. L., & Dweck, C. S. (1999). Person versus process praise and criticism: Implications for contingent self-worth and coping. *Developmental Psychology, 35,* 835–847.

Karwoski, L., Leslie, C., Ilardi, M. G. and Stephen, S. (2006). On the integration of cognitive-behavioural therapy for depression and positive psychology. *Journal of Cognitive Psychotherapy, 20*(2), 159–170.

Kavale, K. A. (2007). Quantitative research synthesis: Meta-analysis of research on meeting special educational needs. In L. Florian (Ed.), *Handbook of Special Education* (pp. 207–221). London: Sage.

Kazdin, A. E. (2000). Psychotherapy for children and adolescents. In A. E. Bergin & S. L. Garfield (Eds.), *Handbook of Play Therapy and Behaviour Change* (4th edn.). New York: Wiley.

Kearns, H. (2005). Exploring the experiential learning of special educational needs coordinators. *Journal of In-Service Education, 31*(1), 131–150.

Knight, T. (2001). Longitudinal development of educational theory: Democracy and the classroom. *Journal of Education Policy, 16*(3), 249–263.

Knowsley Council (2008). *Future Schooling in Knowsley – A Strategy for Change 2008–2010.* Knowsley: Knowsley Council.

Lamb, B. (2009). *The Lamb Inquiry: Special Educational Needs and Parental Confidence.* London: DCSF.

Lancaster, Y. P., & Broadbent, V. (2003). *Listening to Young Children.* Maidenhead: Open University Press.

Lanyado, M., & Horne, A. (2009). *The Handbook of Child and Adolescent Psychotherapy: Psychoanalytic Approaches* (2nd edn.). London: Routledge

Laslett, R. (1998). *Changing Perceptions: Emotional and Behavioural Difficulties since 1945.* Maidstone: AWCEBD.

Lave, J., & Wenger, E. (1990). *Situated Learning: Legitimate Peripheral Participation.* Cambridge: Cambridge University Press.

LaVigna, G. W., & Donnellan, A. M. (1986). *Alternatives to Punishment: Solving Behaviour Problems with Non-aversive Strategies.* New York: Irvington Publishers.

Lawson, H. (2003). Pupil participation: Questioning the extent? *SLD Experience, 36,* 31–35.

Lawson, H. (2010). Beyond tokenism: Participation of/with pupils with significant learning difficulties. In R. Rose (Ed.), *Confronting Obstacles to Inclusion – International Responses to Developing Inclusive Schools* (pp. 137–151). London: Routledge.

Leary, M. R. (1999). Making sense of self-esteem. *Current Directions in Psychological Science, 8,* 32–35.

Levitas, R. (2005). *The Inclusive Society? Social Exclusion and New Labour* (2nd edn.). Basingstoke: Palgrave Macmillan.

Lewinsohn, P. M., & Clarke, G. N. (1999). Psychosocial treatments for adolescent depression. *Clinical Psychology Review, 19*(3), 329–342.

Lewis, A., Davison, I., Ellins, J., Niblett, L., Parsons, S., Robertson, C. et al. (2007). The experiences of disabled children and their families. *British Journal of Special Education, 34*(4), 189–195.

Lewis, I., & Vulliamy, G. (1980). Warnock or warlock? The sorcery of definitions: The limitations of the report on special education. *Educational Review, 32*(1), 3–10.

Lewis, M., & Brooks-Gunn, J. (1978). Self-knowledge and emotional development. In M. Lewis & L. A. Rosenblum (Eds.), *The Development of Affect* (pp. 205–226). New York: Plenum.

Lewis, R., & Doorlag, D. (2006). *Teaching Special Students in General Education Classrooms* (7th edn.). Upper Saddle River, NJ: Pearson Prentice-Hall.

Lindsay, G. (2007). Educational psychology and the effectiveness of inclusion/mainstreaming. *British Journal of Educational Psychology*, *77*, 1–24.

Lindsay, G., Pather, S., & Strand, S. (2006). *Special Educational Needs and Ethnicity: Issues of Over- and Under-representation*. Research Report RR757. London: DfES.

Living Heritage (2010). *Going to School: The 1870 Act*. Retrieved 23 September 2010 from: http://www.parliament.uk/about/living-heritage/transformingsociety/livinglearning/school/overview/1870educationact/.

Lundy, L. (2007). 'Voice' is not enough: Conceptualising Article 12 of the United Nations Convention on the Rights of the Child. *British Educational Research Journal*, *33*(6), 927–942.

Lunt, I., & Norwich, B. (1999). *Can Effective Schools be Inclusive Schools?* London: Institute of Education, University of London.

MacBeath, J., Galton, M., Steward, S., MacBeath, A., & Page, C. (2006). *The Costs of Inclusion: A Study of Inclusion Policy and Practice in English Primary, Secondary and Special Schools*. Cambridge: University of Cambridge, Faculty of Education.

MacDonald, S. J. (2010). Towards a social reality of dyslexia. *British Journal of Learning Disabilities*, *38*, 271–279.

Mace, F. C., Lalli, J. S., & Pinter-Lalli, P. (1991). Functional analysis and treatment of aberrant behaviour. *Research in Development Disabilities*, *12*(2), 155–180.

Marsh, H. (1985). Self-concept: Its multifaceted, hierarchical structure. *Educational Psychologist*, *20*, 107–123.

Marsh, H. (1987). The big-fish-little-pond-effect on academic self-concept. *Journal of Educational Psychology*, *79*, 280–295.

Marsh, H., & Yeung, A. S. (1997). Causal effects of academic self-concept on academic achievement: Structural equation models of longitudinal data. *Journal of Educational Psychology*, *89*, 41–54.

Martin, W., & Rezai-Rashti, G. (2009). Relationships between boys, teachers and education. In J. Budde & I. Mammes (Eds.), *Jungenforschung empirisch zwischen Schule, männlichem Habitus und Peerkultur* (pp. 191–204). Wiesbaden: VS Verlag für Sozialwissenschaften.

Maslow, A. (1954). *Motivation and Personality*. New York: Harper & Brothers.

May, H. (2004). Interpreting pupil participation into practice: Contributions of the SEN Code of Practice (2001). *Journal of Research in Special Educational Needs*, *4*(2), 67–73.

McNab, I. (2009). Collaborative consultation: Psychologists and teachers working together. In P. Hick, R. Kershner, & P. Farrell (Eds.), *Psychology for Inclusive Education: New Directions for Theory and Practice* (pp. 139–150). Abingdon: Routledge.

MENCAP (2007). *Bullying Wrecks Lives: The Experiences of Children and Young People with a Learning Disability*. Retrieved from: http://www.mencap.org.uk/.

Methven, S. (2009). Commentary: A positive approach to risk requires person-centred thinking. *Tizard Learning Disability Review*, *14*(4), 25–27.

Ministry of Education (1945). *The Handicapped Pupils and School Health Service Regulations 1945*. London: Ministry of Education.

Mitchell, D. (2008). *What Really Works in Special and Inclusive Education? Using Evidence-based Teaching Strategies*. Abingdon: Routledge.

Mittler, P. (2000). *Working Towards Inclusion*. London: Fulton.

Moss, P. (2007). Bringing politics into the nursery: Early childhood education as a democratic practice. *European Early Childhood Education Research Journal*, *15*(1), 5–20.

Mowat, J. (2009). The inclusion of pupils perceived as having SEBD in mainstream schools: A focus upon learning. *Support for Learning*, 24(4), 159–169.

Mueller, C. M., & Dweck, C. S. (1998). Praise for intelligence can undermine children's motivation and performance. *Journal of Personality and Social Psychology*, 75, 33–52.

Muijs, D. (2010). Effectiveness and disadvantage in education: Can a focus on effectiveness aid equity in education? In C. Raffo, A. Dyson, H. Gunter, D. Hall, L. Jones, & A. Kalambouka (Eds.), *Education and Poverty in Affluent Countries* (pp. 85–96). London: Routledge.

Nash, T., & Norwich, B. (2010). The initial training of teachers to teach children with special educational needs: A national survey of English Post Graduate Certificate of Education programmes. *Teaching and Teacher Education*, 26, 1471–1480.

National Assembly for Wales (2006). *Inclusion and Pupil Support*. National Assembly for Wales Circular #47/2006. Retrieved from: http://new.wales.gov.uk/dcells/publications/policy_strategy_and_planning/schools/inclusionandpupilsupport/guidance/introduction/introductioninclusionpupil2.pdf?lang=en.

Neill, A. S. (1962). *Summerhill*. London: Gollancz.

Neill, M., Allen, J., Woodhead, N., Sanderson, H., Reid, S., & Erwin, L. (2009). A positive approach to risk requires person-centred thinking. *Tizard Learning Disability Review*, 14(4), 17–24.

NICE (National Institute for Health and Clinical Excellence) (2008). *Promoting Children's Social and Emotional Wellbeing in Primary Education*. London: NICE.

Noble, T., & McGrath, H. (2008). The positive educational practices framework: A tool for facilitating the work of educational psychologists is promoting pupil wellbeing. *Educational and Child Psychology*, 25(2), 119–133.

Northern Ireland Office (2006). Press release. Retrieved from: http://www.nio.gov.uk/media-detail.htm?newsID=12831.

Norwich, B. (2007). *Dilemmas of Difference, Inclusion and Disability: International Perspectives and Future Directions*. London: Routledge.

Norwich, B. (2010). Can we envisage the end of special educational needs? Has it outlived its usefulness? *Psychology of Education Review*, 32(2), 13–20.

NUT (National Union of Teachers) (1962). *The Education of Maladjusted Children*. London: NUT.

Ofsted (Office for Standards in Education) (2000). *Educational Inclusion: Guidance for Inspectors and Schools*. London: Ofsted.

Ofsted (Office for Standards in Education) (2006). *Inclusion: Does it Matter Where Pupils are Taught? Provision and Outcomes in Different Settings for Pupils with Learning Difficulties and Disabilities*. London: Ofsted.

Ofsted (Office for Standards in Education) (2009). *The Annual Report of Her Majesty's Chief Inspector of Education, Children's Services and Skills. 2008/09*. London: Ofsted.

Ofsted (Office for Standards in Education) (2010). *The Special Educational Needs and Disability Review: A Statement is Not Enough*. Manchester: Ofsted.

Ollendick, T., & King, N. (1998). Empirically supported treatments for children with phobic and anxiety disorders. *Journal of Clinical and Child Psychology*, 61(2), 235–247.

O'Mara, A. J., Marsh, H. W., Craven, R. G., & Debus, R. L. (2006). Do self-concept interventions make a difference? A synergistic blend of construct validation and meta-analysis. *Educational Psychologist*, 41, 181–206.

Orkney Council (2011). *Defining Inclusion*. Retrieved 5 May 2011 from: http://www.orkney.gov.uk/Service-Directory/D/Defining-Inclusion.htm.

Orwell, G. (1947). Politics and the English language. In G. Orwell (Ed.), *Essays*. London: Penguin Classics.

Owens, K. (1997). Six myths about self-esteem. *Journal of Invitational Theory and Practice, 4,* 115–129.

Parkin, J. (2007). Stop feminising our schools – our boys are suffering. *Daily Mail,* 31 January.

Pattison, S., Rowland, N., Cromarty, K., Richards, K., Jenkins, P., Cooper, M. et al. (2007). *Counselling in Schools: A Research Study into Services for Children and Young People in Wales.* Lutterworth: BACP.

Perry, E., & Francis, B. (2010). *The Social Class Gap for Educational Achievement: A Review of the Literature.* London: RSA.

Pettitt, B. (2003). *Effective Joint Working between Child and Adolescent Mental Health Services (CAMHS) and Schools.* Research Report RR142. London: DH.

Priestley, M., Miller, K., Barrett, L., & Wallace, C. (2010). Teaching learning communities and educational change in Scotland: The Highland experience. *British Educational Research Journal, 37*(2), 265–284.

Print, M. (2007). Citizenship education and youth participation in democracy. *British Journal of Educational Studies, 55*(3), 325–345.

Public Health Institute of Scotland (2003). *Needs Assessment Report on Child and Adolescent Mental Health.* Edinburgh: Public Health Institute of Scotland.

Pumfrey, P. D. (2010). United Kingdom special educational needs: Reflections and current concerns. *Psychology of Education Review, 32*(2), 3–12.

Quicke, J., & Winter, C. (1994). Labelling and learning an interactionist perspective. *Support for Learning, 9*(1), 16–22.

Quinn, P., & Chan, S. (2009). Secondary school students' preferences for location, format of counselling and gender of counsellor: A replication study based in Northern Ireland. *Counselling and Psychotherapy Research, 9*(3), 204–209.

Randall, P., & Parker, J. (1999). *Supporting Families of Children with Autism.* Chichester: Wiley.

Rapple, B. A. (1994). Payment by results: An example of assessment in elementary education from nineteenth century Britain. *Education Policy Analysis Archives, 2*(1). Retrieved from: http://epaa.asu.edu/epaa/v2n1.html.

Reasoner, R., & Lane, M. (2007). *Parenting with Purpose: Five Ways to Raising Children with Values and Vision.* New York: Personhood Press.

Riddick, B. (1996). *Living with Dyslexia.* London: Routledge.

Riddick, B. (2000). An examination of the relationship between labelling and stigmatisation with special reference to dyslexia. *Disability and Society, 14*(4), 653–667.

Riddick, B. (2010). *Living with Dyslexia: The Social and Emotional Consequences of Specific Learning Difficulty/Disability* (2nd edn.). London: Routledge.

Riddick, B., Farmer, M., & Sterling, C. (1997). *Students and Dyslexia.* London: Whurr Publishers.

Riddick, B., Wolfe, J., & Lumsden, D. (2003). *Dyslexia: A Practical Guide for Teachers and Parents.* London: David Fulton.

Rigolon, A., & Alloway, M. (2011). Children and their development as a starting point: A new way to think about the design of elementary schools. *Educational and Child Psychology, 28*(1), 64–76.

Rinaldi, W. (1992). *The Social Use of Language Programme (SULP).* Windsor: NFER-Nelson.

Robertson, J., Emerson, E., Hatton, C., Elliott, J., McIntosh, B., Swift, P. et al. (2005). *The Impact of Person Centred Planning for People with Intellectual Disabilities in England: A Summary of Findings.* Lancaster: Lancaster University, Institute for Health Research.

Robins, R. W., & Trzesniewski, K. H. (2005). Self-esteem development across the lifespan. *Current Directions in Psychological Science, 14,* 158–162.

Robinson, K. (2010). 'Changing Paradigms' Lecture (RSA) (Royal Society for the Encouragement of Arts, Manufactures and Commerce). Retrieved from: http://www.youtube.com/watch?v—CbdS4hSa0s.

Rogers, C. (1969). *Freedom to Learn: A View of what Education Might Become.* Columbus, OH: C.E. Merrill Pub. Co.

Rose, J. (2009). *Identifying and Teaching Children and Young People with Dyslexia and Learning Difficulties.* London: DCSF.

Rosenham, D. (1973). On being sane in insane places. *Science, 179*(4070), 250–258.

Routledge, M., Sanderson, H., & Greig, R. (2002). *Planning with People Towards Person-centred Approaches: The Development of Guidance on Person-centred Planning for the English Department of Health.* London: DH.

Rowley, H., & Dyson, A. (2011). Academies in the public interest – a contradiction in terms? In H. M. Gunter (Ed.), *The State and Education Policy: The Academies Programme* (pp. 79–91). London: Continuum.

Rudd, T., Colligan, F., & Naik, R. (2006). *Learner Voice.* Bristol: Futurelab.

Ryan, R. L., & Deci, E. L. (2000). Intrinsic and extrinsic motivations: Classic definitions and new directions. *Contemporary Educational Psychology, 25*(1), 68–81.

Sainsbury, C. (2009). *A Martian in the Playground.* London: Lucky Duck Books.

Salt, T. (2010). *Independent Review of Services for Children and Young People (0–19) with Speech, Language and Communication Needs.* London: DCSF.

Sanderson, H. (2000). *Person-centred Planning: Key Features and Approaches.* York: Joseph Rowntree Foundation.

Saunders, L. (2011). Road crashes and war-mongering: Why the notion of 'impact' in research is wrong. *Research Intelligence: British Educational Research Association, 114*, 16–17.

Schick, T., & Vaughn, L. (2010). *Doing Philosophy: An Introduction Through Thought Experiments* (4th edn.). Boston, MA: McGraw-Hill Higher Education.

Schools Analysis and Research Division (2009). *Deprivation and Education: The Evidence on Pupils in England, Foundation Stage to Key Stage 4.* London: DCSF.

Scottish Executive (2005). *Supporting Children's Learning: Code of Practice.* Retrieved from: http://www.additionalsupportneeds.org.uk/downloads/asncode.pdf.

Seale, J., & Nind, M. (2010). Access and the concept of risk: Preventing bad things from happening or making good things happen? In J. Seale & M. Nind (Eds.), *Understanding and Promoting Access for People with Learning Difficulties: Seeing the Opportunities and Challenges of Risk* (pp. 165–186). London: Routledge.

SENDIST (Special Educational Needs and Disability Tribunal) (2003). *Special Educational Needs and Disability Tribunal Annual Report 2002–03.* London: SENDIST.

Shavelson, R. J., Hubner, J. J., & Stanton, G. C. (1976). Self-concept: Validation of construct interpretations. *Review of Educational Research, 46*, 407–441.

Silverman, W. K., Kurtines, W. M., Ginsburg, G. S., Weems, C. F., Lumpkin, P. W., & Carmichael, D. H. (1999). Treating anxiety disorders in children with group cognitive behaviour therapy: A randomised clinical trial. *Journal of Consulting and Clinical Psychology, 67*, 995–1003.

Slee, R. (2001). Driven to the margins: Disabled students, inclusive schooling and the politics of possibility. *Cambridge Journal of Education, 31*(3), 385–397.

Social Exclusion Unit (2004). *Tackling Social Exclusion: Taking Stock and Looking to the Future. Emerging Findings.* London: ODPM Publications.

Spence, S., Donovan, C., & Brechman-Toussaint, M. (2000). The treatment of childhood social phobia: The effectiveness of a social skills training-based cognitive behavioural intervention with and without parental involvement. *Journal of Child Psychology and Psychiatry, 41*, 713–726.

Squires, G. (1996). *The Use of Praise as a Tool in the Classroom Management of Behaviour.* Unpublished MSc thesis, University of Manchester, Manchester.

Squires, G. (2001). Using cognitive behavioural psychology with groups of pupils to improve self-control of behaviour. *Educational Psychology in Practice, 17*(4), 317–335.

Squires, G. (2002). *Changing Thinking and Feeling to Change Behaviour: Cognitive Interventions.* Ainsdale: Positive Behaviour Management.

Squires, G. (2010). Countering the argument that educational psychologists need specific training to use cognitive behavioural therapy. *Emotional and Behavioural Difficulties, 4,* 279–294.

Squires, G., & Dunsmuir, S. (2011). Embedding cognitive behavioural therapy training in practice: Facilitators and barriers for trainee educational psychologists (TEPs). *Educational Psychology in Practice, 27*(2), 117–132.

Squires, G., & Farrell, P. (2006). Educational psychology in England and Wales. In S. R. Jimerson, T. D. Oakland, & P. T. Farrell (Eds.), *The Handbook of International School Psychology* (p. 90). Thousand Oaks, CA: Sage.

Stallard, P. (2002). *Think Good – Feel Good: A Cognitive Behaviour Therapy Workbook for Children and Young People.* Chichester: Wiley.

Stallard, P. (2005). *A Clinician's Guide to Think Good – Feel Good: Using CBT with Children and Young People.* Chichester: Wiley.

Strawbridge, S., & Woolfe, R. (2010). Counselling psychology: Origins, developments and challenges. In R. Woolfe, S. Strawbridge, B. Douglas, & W. Dryden (Eds.), *Handbook of Counselling Psychology* (3rd edn., pp. 3–22). London: Sage.

Stronach, I., & Piper, H. (2008). Can liberal education make a comeback? The case of 'relational touch' at Summerhill School. *American Educational Research Journal, 45*(1), 6–37.

Swann, W. B., Wenzlaff, R. M., Krull, D. S., & Pelham, B. W. (1992). Allure of negative feedback: Self-verification strivings among depressed persons. *Journal of Abnormal Psychology, 101,* 293–306.

Thomas, G., & Loxley, A. (2007). *Deconstructing Special Education and Constructing Inclusion* (2nd edn.). Maidenhead: Open University Press.

Thorndike, R. M. (1997). The origins of intellectual assessment. In D. P. Flanagan, J. L. Genshaft, & P. L. Harrison (Eds.), *Contemporary Intellectual Assessment* (pp. 3–16). London: Guilford Press.

Tobias, A. (2009). Supporting students with autistic spectrum disorder in mainstream school: A parent and student perspective. *Educational Psychology in Practice, 25*(2), 151–165.

Tomlinson, S. (1982). *A Sociology of Special Education.* London: Routledge & Kegan Paul.

Tough, P. (2008). *Whatever it Takes: Geoffrey Canada's Quest to Change Harlem and America.* Boston, MA: Houghton Mifflin.

Tribunals Service (2009). *Special Educational Needs and Disability Tribunal: Annual Report 2008–2009.* London: Tribunals Service.

Turgenev, I. (1860). *First Love.* London: Penguin Classics.

Turnbull, A., Turnbull, R., Erwin, E., & Soodak, L. (2006). *Families, Professionals, and Exceptionality: Positive Outcomes through Partnerships and Trust.* Upper Saddle River, NJ: Pearson Prentice-Hall.

Underwood Report (1955). *Report of the Committee on Maladjusted Children.* London: Her Majesty's Stationery Office.

UNESCO (United Nations Educational, Scientific and Cultural Organization) (1994a). *Final Report: World Conference on Special Needs Education: Access and Quality.* Paris: UNESCO.

UNESCO (United Nations Educational, Scientific and Cultural Organization) (1994b). *The Salamanca Statement and Framework for Action on Special Needs Education.* Salamanca: UNESCO.

UNESCO (United Nations Educational, Scientific and Cultural Organization) (2000). *The Dakar Framework for Action. Education for All: Meeting our Collective Commitments.* Paris: UNESCO.

United Nations (1989). *Convention on the Rights of the Child.* New York: United Nations.

Visser, J. (2003). *A Study of Children and Young People who Present Challenging Behaviour.* London: Ofsted.

Vygotsky, L. S. (1978). *Mind and Society: The Development of Higher Mental Processes.* Cambridge, MA: Harvard University Press.

Wampold, B. E. (2001). *The Great Psychotherapy Debate: Models, Methods and Findings.* Mahwah, NJ: Erlbaum.

Ward, H. (2009). Lamb backs parents in damning report. *Times Educational Supplement,* 18 December.

Warnock, M. (1978). *Special Educational Needs: Report of the Committee of Enquiry into the Education of Handicapped Children and Young People.* London: Her Majesty's Stationery Office.

Wasserman, J. D., & Tulsky, D. S. (2005). A history of intelligence assessment. In D. P. Flanagan & P. L. Harrison (Eds.), *Contemporary Intellectual Assessment* (2nd edn.). London: Guilford Press.

Weare, K. (2010). Mental health and social and emotional learning: Evidence, principles, tensions, balances. *Advances in School Mental Health Promotion, 3,* 5–17.

Weare, K., & Markham, W. (2005). What do we know about promoting mental health through schools? *Promotion and Education, 3*(4), 118–122.

Webster, R., Blatchford, P., Bassett, P., Brown, P., Martin, C., & Russell, A. (2010). Double standards and first principles: Framing teaching assistant support for pupils with special educational needs. *European Journal of Special Educational Needs, 25*(4), 319–336.

Webster-Wright, A. (2009). Reframing professional development through understanding authentic professional learning. *Review of Educational Research, 29*(2), 702–739.

Wedell, K. (2008). Confusion about inclusion: Patching up or system change? *British Journal of Special Education, 35*(3), 127–135.

Welsh Assembly Government (2008). *School-based Counselling Services in Wales: A National Strategy.* Cardiff: Welsh Assembly Government.

Wildemeersch, D., & Vandenabeele, J. (2007). Relocating learning as a democratic practice: Increased emphasis in citizenship education. In R. van der Veen, D. Wildemeersch, J. Youngblood, & V. Marsick (Eds.), *Democratic Practices as Learning Opportunities* (pp. 19–32). Rotterdam: Sense.

Wilkin, A., Archer, T., Ridley, K., Fletcher-Campbell, F., & Kinder, K. (2005). *Admissions and Exclusions of Pupils with Special Educational Needs.* Research Report RR608. Nottingham: DfES.

Wilkinson, R., & Pickett, K. (2009). *The Spirit Level: Why More Equal Societies Almost Always Do Better.* London: Penguin Books.

Wilson, J. (2007). How shall we define 'handicap'? *British Journal of Special Education, 11*(2), 33–35.

Wilson, P. (2004). *Young Minds in our Schools: A Guide for Teachers and Others Working in School.* London: Karnac.

Youell, B. (2006). *The Learning Environment.* London: Karnac.

Zimmerman, B. (2008). Investigating self-regulation and motivation: Historical background, methodological developments, and future prospects. *American Educational Research Journal, 45*(1), 166–183.

Index

**INCLUSION
Developing an Effective Whole
School Approach**

Alison Ekins and Peter Grimes

9780335236046 (Paperback)
2009

eBook also available

This book examines and offers solutions to the challenges faced by schools in ensuring that all students are enjoying, participating and achieving in education. The authors argue that self evaluation lies at the heart of truly inclusive school development.

The book focuses on supporting schools in understanding and using school based systems and processes in a joined up, meaningful and strategic way to impact positively upon the progress and participation of all pupils.

Key features:

- Responds to the day to day needs of the SENCO, teacher, leader
- Provides case studies, examples, templates and models
- Focuses on supporting schools in understanding and using school based systems and processes in a joined up, meaningful and strategic way to impact positively upon the progress and participation of all pupils.

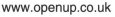www.openup.co.uk

OPEN UNIVERSITY PRESS
McGraw - Hill Education

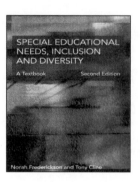

**SPECIAL EDUCATIONAL NEEDS,
INCLUSION AND DIVERSITY**
Second Edition

Norah Frederickson and Tony Cline

9780335221462 (Paperback)
2009

eBook also available

For many readers, the first edition of this book became the textbook
on special educational needs. The new edition builds on this, offering
a balance between theory, research and practice as well as a unique
analysis of the implications of the effects of linguistic, cultural and
ethnic diversity on special educational needs.

Key features:

- Broader coverage of hot topics which have been the focus of
  recent research, including dyspraxia; the role of genetic factors in
  development, and the contribution of neuroscience to our
  understanding of SEN
- Coverage of the impact of recent legislation and other national
  initiatives in education, including curricular, organizational and
  structural initiatives
- New materials and methods for assessment and teaching

www.openup.co.uk

OPEN UNIVERSITY PRESS
McGraw · Hill Education